LEO'S WAR
From Gaspé To Vimy

LEO'S WAR
From Gaspé To Vimy

GORDON PIMM

PARTNERSHIP PUBLISHERS
Ottawa, Canada

Library and Archives Canada Cataloguing in Publication

Pimm, Gordon H., 1923-

Leo's war : from Gaspé to Vimy / Gordon H. Pimm.

Includes bibliographical references.

ISBN 978-0-9783052-0-8

1. LeBoutillier, Leo — Correspondence. 2. World War, 1914-1918
— Personal narratives, Canadian. 3. Canada. Canadian Army —
Biography. 4. Soldiers — Québec (Province) — Gaspé Peninsula
— Correspondence. 5. Gaspé Peninsula (Québec) — Biography.
I. Title.

D640.P45 2007   940.4'8171479   C2007-901427-5

1 2 3 4 5 6 7 8 9 10

First Edition

TABLE OF CONTENTS

PROLOGUE

I was born in Gaspé in the family home of my mother who was a descendent of John LeBoutillier, one of the early residents of the Gaspé Peninsula. His great granddaughter, Gertie, my mother's unmarried sister, lived there until she died in 1984 when the house was sold to become a Bed and Breakfast and tourist attraction. As a child we would summer there with our cousins, and on rainy days, Aunt Gertie would often send us to the attic to play among the boxes of old toys, uniforms, dressmaking mannequins and assorted paraphernalia the attic contained.

My birth occurred on one of these summer vacations so I never lived in Gaspé and rarely returned as an adult. However, when I finally did take my own children to the family home, I suggested they view the "treasures" of the attic. It was while playing in the attic that my eight-year-old son discovered a Ganongs chocolate box containing his Great Uncle Leo's letters from the Front in World War I.

To our astonishment, Aunt Gertie entrusted the letters to our family. For the next 45 years my wife and I dutifully made sure they were never left behind on our rather frequent moves from house to house during our long life together. We would occasionally open the box and read one or two but there seemed little connection between Leo's life in the trenches in the First World War and my experience in the Canadian Navy in WWII. As our own children knew nothing of war, there seemed little reason to read the entire box but we still honoured Aunt Gertie's trust in me to keep and preserve the letters.

It wasn't until my wife and I decided to visit the Normandy Beaches on the 60th Anniversary of the Allied Invasion that I thought of visiting the Canadian Monument at Vimy where Leo had fought. We stayed at an old Hotel in Arras, and with our adult daughter, who resides in Switzerland, we visited the trenches, battlefield and "no man's land" at the Canadian site of Vimy.

It was a gloomy, rainy day when we walked the same ground on which Leo had fought and suddenly we began to feel his presence. We immediately returned to our Hotel, quickly brought out the random sample of his letters we had thought to bring with us and began to read.

In this setting, under these conditions, the letters came alive and spoke to us as though he were there. We were hypnotized by his words and impressed by his writing talent. He seemed to talk to us over the years about his personal experience as a Canadian solider in a war that continues to defy explanation to the average Canadian.

Shortly after returning to Canada my wife said to me "You have to write Leo's story" and thus this book began.

My first thought was to survey other family members who might have photographs or memories of Uncle Leo. This activity was rewarded with an incredible outpouring of interest, support, letters and pictures.

My initial helper was my sister's son Tim who found in his mother's basement several letters and who helped organize and enter some of this manuscript into the computer. Further family research involved the enthusiastic participation of many of the surviving nieces and nephews, some of whom had, like Aunt Gertie, saved the letters written to their mother or father from Leo.

Leo's brother Bert's son Charles is still a resident of Gaspé and he and his son Matthew continue to operate C. S. LeBoutillier Insurance there. Charles and his wife Betty as well as their son Steven in Toronto and niece Ann in Calgary provided some of the most informative and poignant of the letters included in this book.

They also provided an article that appeared in *Rod and Gun* magazine in 1910 written by the aspiring author sixteen year old Leo. He turns out to be an excellent writer who's writing and publishing career has had a 97-year pause but is now being revived in this book.

The project has resulted in the extended family renewing contact with each other largely through the efforts of Winifred Emmett of Montreal who hosted a family gathering to talk and reminisce about Gaspé summers when we were young. It seems as if Leo's letters have had the same effect on others as he did in person where he was acknowledged by all who knew him as a kind, and loyal friend respectful of and respected by others.

Acknowledgments

I would like to thank the following people without whom this book would not have been possible.

The Canadian National Archives and the Rockcliffe Park branch of the Ottawa Public Library system were extremely helpful to me in finding source material as was the staff of the Library and Archives of the Canadian War Museum.

John Peirce, author and fellow member of the Ottawa Independent Writers Association, gave me the first and best advice for anyone talking of writing a book. " Stop talking and start writing- every day!"

John Wood, author, formerly Director of the National Arts Centre Theatre in Ottawa, read a first draft and made very useful suggestions that have been incorporated into the organization of this material.

Norman Christie, author, publisher and host of the documentary *For King & Empire* read the final manuscript and with extraordinary generosity shared his extensive knowledge of the period described in Leo's letters. He also displayed a unique and helpful familiarity with place names obtained from his many years as Chief Records Officer of the Commonwealth Graves Commission.

Blake Seward, creator of the award-winning High School program *The Lest We Forget Project,* generously provided editing suggestions and shared his experiences gained in supervising student research into the lives of fallen World War I soldiers.

My brothers, Robert, Leo and Arthur, and sister Marjorie shared personal recollections of summers in Gaspe' and memories of stories told about our mother's brother Leo.

Cousins Winifred Emmett, Gwendolyn Gibson, Paul Brassard, Hugh and Charles Whalen, and Charles and Betty LeBoutillier, their son Steven and niece Ann (McCarthy) Scott all contributed memories, pictures and letters as well as enthusiastic support for the project. Steven deserves special thanks for his work in transcribing thirteen 90 year old letters from Leo written in pencil on whatever paper was available to him.

Nephew Tim Lemoyre searched his mother's files and not only provided valuable content, but also typing, research ideas, and web sites along with encouragement.

My good friend Warden McKimm meticulously copy-edited the final manuscript which resulted in a great improvement in the book's readability.

My wife June whose writing and organizational skills match her good nature in working with me on this project would qualify for her co-authorship in any fair analysis of the effort made in producing this book.

Finally I need to acknowledge the enthusiastic support I have received from members of my immediate family, including my daughter Martha, my sons Robert and Matthew, and my granddaughter Notta. Each in their own way contributed time, interest and direct help in support of the idea of my writing a book on my Uncle Leo's letters and in the actual production of the book.

-Gordon Pimm
Ottawa, April 2007

INTRODUCTION

This book is about Leo B. LeBoutillier and his brief military career as a young Canadian soldier during World War I. Known to his fellow soldiers as "Boots," Leo's story is told through sixty personal letters written to his extended family during the war and kept for him at his request. He had written saying that he would not have time to keep a diary and hoped his letters would suffice. Since so much time has elapsed since WWI, the author has included text placing the letters in historical context.

Through Leo's letters we learn much about the transformation of a brave and thoughtful young man adapting to the experience of war. His words also speak for a generation of young Canadians who by their bravery and sacrifice forged a Canadian identity through their part in the Great War.

Leo's attitude toward his home in Canada, the war and his place in it, and his steadfast response to the pitiless conditions of everyday life in the trenches, are vividly revealed in his writing. Despite the work of Censors to restrain the flow of information from the front lines, Leo's letters still manage to portray the intensity of his moment-to-moment life in battle and to get a sense of his experiences as though you are there.

For the Canadian Army during the 1914-18 War, the censorship of letters home from the front was taken very seriously. Every postcard or letter was co-signed on the envelope by a Censor. Soldiers chose among Postcards and Brown Envelopes which were censored at the Regimental level. Green Envelopes were subject to review by Headquarters in England. However, Green Envelopes were usually forwarded so long as they were certified by the letter-writer as conforming to censorship rules. This two-level censorship was not to back-up one system with another but was in place to offer privacy to "other ranks" as non-Officers were referred to. In this way they could share personal feelings with their family and friends.

Perhaps this unusual sensitivity to personal feelings by the Canadian Army arose because the army was largely a civilian militia rather than a professional force. Also, most Canadian units were held together as much as possible from enlistment-to-action. Because so many Canadian soldiers came from small towns, the junior officers to whom the task of censorship fell could well have been next-door neighbours prior to enlistment.

A novel idea was the preprinted postcard where the information the sender did not wish to send was simply crossed-out. Choices on the postcards included phrases such as: *"I am quite well;" "I have been admitted to hospital;" "Sick or wounded;" "I am getting on well;" "I hope to be discharged soon"*. Indeed, having the Censor pre-write your communication for you was certainly the epitome of efficiency in this area. But you still had to pay for the 2¢ stamp.

If you composed your own letter you were admonished not to mention your rank, brigade, the names of places, expected operations, movements or numbers of troop casualties previous to the publication of the official lists, or make specific reference to the morale or physical condition of troops. Given these restrictions it is not surprising that most letters from the front were not very informative nor of a high standard of literacy.

Nevertheless, the letters narrated in this book are not about the war itself. They are instead the letters of a young man "at war" who shares with us his story of survival in terrifying conditions. As one might expect, there is a detectible change in the tone of Leo's letters over time.

The very act of writing seems to have played a unique role in helping him to develop his insight and understanding of the world in which he found himself. It is possible that staying connected by letter to the straightforward world of Canada was integral to his survival.

৪৩

Every letter recounted in this book is real, although punctuation may have been added to improve comprehension, but spelling remains as written. The letters have not been edited for form or content.

At the beginning of each letter, I note the place where the letter was written—something the Censor would not allow Leo to do for himself. Also, where possible, Leo's references to his activities in his letters are matched to what was actually happening in the war as gleaned from other sources.

The recipients of the letters for the most part comprise Leo's parents, brother and sisters who are my grandparents, mother, aunts and uncles.

Leo's mother **Zoë Therése** (1857-1939) usually referred to as "Mama."

Leo's father "Papa" **Charles Sutton LeBoutillier** (1857-1940).

Gertrude-Mary (1883-1984), referred to as Gertie by the family, was the eldest. She never married and became the central figure in the family after her parents' death.

Zadie (1885-1975) the second oldest in the family married Robert Pimm in 1914 and lived with her husband in Alexandria Ontario. Christened Zoë after her mother, she disliked the name and renamed herself Zadie as a young schoolgirl. Zadie and Robert Pimm are the parents of the author, Gordon Pimm.

Marion Bride (1887-1975) married Moise Brassard in Gaspé and lived as the wife of a respected dentist in Gaspé.

Herbert (1888-1964) "Bert" was the eldest boy who remained in Gaspé while operating the family business and the family farm.

Stella (1890-1970) the fourth girl to be born, married Joseph Grogan and moved to Quebec city where Uncle Joe was connected to the lumber trade.

Lauretta (1896-1989), the youngest, married Tim Whalen who worked in timber in partnership with the LeBoutilliers and as a senior employee of a large paper producer.

In addition to his family Leo also wrote to:

Mrs. (Mary) Hodgson who was the sister of Robert Pimm and lived in England.

Alma Kavanaugh, a cousin who joined the Nursing Corps and was sent to England.

Mrs. Amy, Agent for C.S. LeBoutillier Company in Jersey.

PART I

❦

Canada 1914

CHAPTER ONE

Home in Gaspé

Leo B. LeBoutillier joined the 24th Battalion, Victoria Rifles in Montreal on November 3rd 1914. His personnel file is held in the National Archives in Ottawa and describes him as, *"5' 7½ tall (a 1/2 inch taller than average for the Canadian Expeditionary Force), weight 150 lbs., with brown hair streaked with blond with one eyebrow half brown and half blond."*

When Leo enlisted, he was a graduate of Loyola College in Montreal and was employed as a bank clerk in Gaspé Harbour, Quebec. Gaspé Harbour is across the bay from Gaspé Village located at the tip of the Gaspé Peninsula, a distinctive 200-mile long and 70-mile wide projection into the Gulf of St Lawrence. Rising from the sea, it is the northern end of the Appalachian mountain chain, whose northern coast forms the mouth of the St Lawrence River.

Gaspé Village was the centre of the inshore cod fishing industry during the previous century and along with the peninsula's scattered coves and harbours has accommodated to numerous (usually resource based) economic ups-and-downs since its discovery by Europeans in the early 1500's.

In 1914, when Leo's war began, Gaspé Harbour was lined with wharves and warehouses with both sailing ships and steamers anchored in the bay. It looked like most small seaports appeared at the time. For a brief period in the middle of the 19th century the codfish was a large source of protein to the world's population and the Gaspé fishery was a significant supplier. Transportation of dried cod from all sources required a substantial proportion of all British shipping capacity—at that time the largest in the world.

As this industry waned, Gaspé's resourceful inhabitants looked to the development of its forests. Trees in Gaspé were as numerous on land as the codfish had been in the sea; and this resource, unlike others, has not dried up but continues, like background music to each of the booms-and-busts, to this day.

Communications had improved from the previous century. It was no longer the shortest route (in winter) to Upper Canada from Gaspé to go by sea to Boston and then take the train to Toronto. Now the train had a terminus in Gaspé Harbour. Slow and uncertain, the railway was the butt of much criticism, memories of previous travel options having dried up.

The advent of the train meant those in Gaspé's English-speaking majority who could afford it, sent their children to bilingual schools in Quebec City, or to English-speaking schools in Montreal. Leo graduated from the high school program at Loyola College (now Concordia) in Montreal.

Recreation in Gaspé was focused on outdoor activities. Young people skated and played hockey on the frozen inner bay in winter. The gasoline-powered motorboat had reached the area and brought new interest in summer water sports.

Moose hunting was an annual experience for Leo and an entertaining article written by him describing a moose hunt published in a 1910 issue of *Rod and Gun* is reproduced in Appendix A. All of Leo's outdoor pursuits reinforced a high degree of rugged self-reliance that undoubtedly prepared him extremely well for trench warfare in France.

In 1914, Gaspé's cultural climate, including religion, was about evenly balanced between mainly Protestant English speakers, and Catholic French speakers—with a slight edge in favour of English speakers. There was, however, an enormous advantage in economic power held by English speakers.

Leo's surname LeBoutillier is a Jersey name. The island of Jersey, with its neighbours, Guernsey, Sark and Aldernay make up the Channel Islands, British possessions off the French coast of Brittany. Leo was the great grandson of The Hon. John LeBoutillier, an entrepreneur from the Channel Islands, who came to the Gaspé area in the early 1800's. John, with other Jerseymen, organized the inshore Canadian cod fishing industry into a worldwide source for protein.

Leo's unique background is evidenced by the newspaper reports of Leo's military exploits always identifying him as "from a prominent Jersey family." The "B" in Leo's name stands for Belleau—his mother's maiden name. The Belleau's were also a prominent Quebec City family who traced their roots to a member of the famed Carignan

Salieres Regiment who remained in Canada in 1668, when that unit returned to France.

The Jersey descendants who lived in Gaspé shared both Catholic and Protestant faiths and spoke both French and English. They bridged the cultural divide, and having inherited significant wealth, they lived a life of privilege. However, what Leo could not have foreseen were the dramatic changes soon coming to Gaspé's culture. French speakers who today enjoy 90% of Gaspé's cultural and economic influence, now dominate the area.

The world that Leo yearns to return to in his letters was for him quiet and slow to change. Although Gaspé was in transition, economic movement was so gradual that Leo had no trouble adapting. Social, linguistic and cultural change was hardly perceptible. "Dear old Gaspé," as Leo often refers to his home, was dear to him for a number of reasons. Gaspé had then and retains now some of the most incredible scenic beauty that the harshness of its climate only seems to enhance. Leo had reasonable prosperity, a multitude of friends, and a dignified role in the Gaspé community. His future was very bright—if only he could return from the war alive.

CHAPTER TWO

Canada's Army

In 1914, Canada was nominally independent. Along with other British colonial possessions, Canada had been granted legislative independence by British Statute in 1867 and reclassified as a Dominion, but remaining legally a colony. Few Canadians, but most Britons recognized this distinction. It was not until 1931 that the *Statute of Westminster* severed most of England's legal control over Canada and the severance of the final legislative connection was not completed until 1982. All that remains now of official English influence is Her Majesty Queen Elizabeth's role as "Queen of Canada" with no connection to her duties as Queen of England, and membership in the British Commonwealth.

In consequence, in 1914 no declaration of war was required of Canada to enter the war, however Canadians like Leo had no doubt where their duty lay. The reaction to the war in Canada was as mixed as its culturally divided make-up might have predicted. Of the population of seven million Canadians in 1914, two million were of French descent, and the balance were British and North European.

When war came and recruiting started, a high proportion of those volunteering first were "old country people" who had been born in England. Some had arrived in Canada only a few months before the war began and many quickly enlisted, perhaps, as an opportunity to get a "free" trip home to visit relatives.

In the beginning no one expected the war to last more than six months.

The response to the "call to arms" from western Canada was especially positive. This was the area recently populated by settlers responding to cheap land promotions from the Canadian railways. The railways had received land grants from the government as an incentive to build the transcontinental rail link. This land was used to promote immigration in anticipation of shipping whatever the settler might produce.

This population was understandably pro British, not the least because largely, they were, British. The enlistment roles filled faster than anyone had predicted.

The First Division assembled at Valcartier that was a hastily constructed mobilization centre near Quebec City. Thirty percent of the recruits came from western Canada. In central and maritime Canada recruiting results were positive but not nearly so.

In Quebec, English speaking recruits came out in force as elsewhere in Canada, but French Canadian participation was largely limited to those from larger cities who had a familiarization with the English language. Additional French speaking recruits came from the Canadian born descendents of what had been a vibrant military tradition having its origin in France.

Only one unit, the 22nd Regiment, popularly known as the Vandoos, was permitted to work in French. In other Quebec raised units the working language was English. All communication with larger formations for everybody was in the working language of the army—English.

The military and political establishment in Canada, until very recently, had always been negatively concerned with what was called the establishment of a parallel army, one English speaking and the other French speaking. In 1914 and during the war a unilingual policy was in effect.

Leo LeBoutillier was one of those who identified with Imperial Britain. He was by social class and economic status a member of an elite who lived in an outpost of English influence at the tip of the Gaspé peninsula.

Leo joined the army on November 3rd, 1914 in Montreal as a Private. The unit was the 24th Battalion Victoria Rifles, organized in October 1914 under the command of Lt. Col. J.A. Gunn. As an organization it had it's genesis as The Beaver Lacrosse Club formed in 1861, whose members had assumed a military role in resisting incursions into Canada from the Fenian raids from The United States.

The 24th recruited and had its initial training in Montreal and left on the S.S. Cameronia on May 11th, 1915 for England, arriving on May 20th. It comprised 42 officers and 1,089 other ranks, Private Leo LeBoutillier being one of them.

Montrealers had adopted the 24th as their own, and as the battalion tried to march to the docks to embark, interference from the enthusiastic crowds was so complete that Lt. Col. Gunn had finally to abandon marching and tell everyone to make their way to the docks on their own. Most made it to the ship before sailing, but some had to entrain for Quebec and join the ship there.

An excerpt of Leo's letter written to his mother on May 13th, 1915 describes this event.

"Monday (May 11th) reveille sounded at 4:30. The last notes were not finished before the barracks was in a howl, everybody began yelling and singing and kept it up until breakfast. After we had something to eat we all felt better and still made more noise. The morning was spent packing; we were confined to barracks all day so couldn't get out. In the afternoon we sat in the windows of our rooms and called out to everybody, and sang songs. At 7:15 the people began to gather on Peel St. at Metcalfe, I made out Charlie in the crowd and he managed to get a letter to me, but not from home, which I expected. 8:45 we marched out in the street in Platoons. The signaling section together and were cheered and clapped over and over again. The Police soon lost control of the crowd and we had an awful time. They crowded around us like flies and when we got the order to form fours and march off we couldn't get into fours. My, my, it was some send off and most likely you won't see a word of it in the papers.

We marched down Metcalfe St. and when we got to St. Catherine's we couldn't push our way through. We marched in fours, two abreast, and single file. People crowded into the ranks and walked with us. Everybody cheering and clapping and shaking your hand and wishing you "good luck". Well, they all went mad and that's all. Girls would throw their arms around you and kiss you "good bye" never having seen you before, cry all over you and wish you "good luck". We pushed our way down St. Catherine St. having an awful time of it. Men would walk along side and beg to carry your kit for you saying you would have to carry it far enough before you get back. After shaking hands with at least 3,000 people we arrived at St. Lawrence Main St. and marched down. When we arrived down near the docks the crowd, I think, was still greater. Every pretty girl I would hold out my hand to and say "good bye" as if we had been old pals. They would take your arm and walk along the way until they got jammed up in the crowd and left behind. I saw some girls I knew and boys who went to Loyola also Douglas Annett and the family, but any amount of others who I know were down I never saw. You could only make out the ones on the inside when we arrived at the dock. We marched in one by one and left the crowd cheering and waving, flapping hats, handkerchiefs and whatever they had. One girl wanted me to take her ring and wear it but I wouldn't take it."

CHAPTER THREE
Sam Hughes

The First Division of the Canadian Expeditionary Force embarked for England in October 1914, three months after the declaration of war. In 1914, Canada's permanent force army was just 3,000 men. By October, more than 30,000 men were in uniform, and along with over 3,000 horses, they left for England. This was a remarkable military build-up in any circumstance, let alone within the undersized population of Canada.

The man in charge was Sam Hughes, the cabinet Minister of Militia during Sir Robert Borden's Conservative government (1911-1920). Sam Hughes served in that post from 1911 to 1916, a remarkable tenure. Yet in 1916 Borden, who had appointed Hughes and supported him, abruptly dismissed Hughes after an open challenge to the Prime Minster's authority.

Hughes has been described as a religious bigot unpopular with French Canadians, irrational and stubborn, among other uncomplimentary assessments. One cabinet colleague even declared him to be insane. He may have been wholly or partly what was said of him, but Hughes was a committed nationalist and his aim was to make Canada a significant national force within the British Empire. For Hughes, commitment had to be complete and total, and his energy matched this determination.

The part that Sam Hughes played is relevant to Leo's story because he, more than anyone, insisted that Canada's contribution to the war maintain a unified Canadian identity. Beyond the crucial military achievements contributed by Canadian soldiers during the War, most historians consider the enduring "Canadian identity" resulting from these contributions as the most significant outcome of Canada's participation in the War. It was Hughes's dogged determination to maintain Canadian soldiers together in battle that led to this historical development.

Hughes arrived in England ahead of his troops, and as soon as he arrived he became a burr under the saddle of those in Britain conducting the war. He demanded recognition for Canadians and insisted on keeping Canadian units together as much as he could. To the embarrassment of both the Canadian and British governments, Hughes interfered with senior military promotions, particularly on behalf of his son, and insisted on equipment decisions in the face of objections from those using them, in particular the Canadian-made Ross rifle.

This gun was accurate but heavy and it jammed in the presence of dirt. It was finally replaced in 1916 and sent to the Royal Navy where mud did not loom as large as in Flanders.

For those who say the most effective advertising is intrusive, grating and infuriating, then Hughes qualified as the best advertisement Canada could have. Indeed, he could not be ignored and finally became so great an irritant that Borden felt he had to remove Hughes from his Cabinet. However, Hughes retained his seat as a Member of Parliament and continued to voice his forceful opinions in the House of Commons and for many years after the war through the newspaper he owned.

As Minister of Militia, Hughes had been preparing for war since 1911 by organizing cadet corps and militia units so that when war came, Canadian forces would come out-of-the gate running. Arguing that mobilization plans were too slow for his liking, he scrapped the Military professional's plans and reorganized the army along militia lines. He appointed himself a Colonel, and shortly thereafter, a Major General. Hughes was questioned for rapidly promoting his son, personal friends and associates to senior military ranks. When Britain asked for help with a garrison to guard Bermuda, his response was to send the Royal Canadian Regiment, his only permant infantry force, thereby assuring himself of a free hand to reorganize the Canadian Expeditionary Force in his own mold.

Patriotic rallies, parades and brass bands rallied young men to the promised adventure. If you hesitated it might be too late. The normal impediments to joining the army did not exist for the potential recruit. You needed to be 5' 4" without flat feet—all else was irrelevant.

Under Hughes energetic leadership, everything was happening at once. A new mobilization centre was built in thirty days—or almost

built (as the earliest arrivals discovered). Within a few weeks of joining up, transportation was organized, and the new recruits were
taken to an embarkation point. Newspapers, speeches by public fig-
ures, and church sermons throughout the land transmitted Hughes
sense of passionate urgency. If you were between 15 and 44 years of
age you had no doubt where your duty lay.

Hughes felt it was vitally important for Canada's military identity that all new recruits be equipped with Canadian-made rifles,
uniforms, boots, ammunition belts, motor trucks, and wagons.
Unfortunately, much of this equipment was later found to be unsuitable and Hughes was roundly criticized for zealously advocating
national identity over effective equipment.

In the pre-war excitement generated by Hughes's focus on recruit-
ment, young Canadians could find no reason to delay joining up.
Hughes had thought of an answer for every anti-war objection and
all opposition was swept aside in a tide of grand hubris—the nation
rallied to action by brass bands and parades.

If Leo LeBoutillier fell under the spell of Hughes's rush to the co-
lours it would not be surprising. Just 20 years old, Leo had recently
completed his education; he was by all accounts like most of the
young men of his generation, believing in honesty, right thinking,
honour and duty.

Nevertheless, Sam Hughes had competition for the services of
the young men of Canada. It came from his own government, who,
while supporting Hughes in his recruiting efforts, were also encouraging those employed in agriculture to remain on the farms.
The Canadian government saw food production as equally important to manufacturing goods for war and recruiting soldiers. Leo's
brother Bert, who was older, operated the family business including
the family farm in Gaspé. There was never any question that Bert
was available for the army. First his eyesight did not reach military
standards; second, his country and family needed him to remain in
Gaspé to manage the farm.

SECOND DIVISION
CANADIAN EXPEDITIONARY FORCE

Comprised of 20,000 men organized into three Brigades

4TH BRIGADE		5TH BRIGADE		6TH BRIGADE
18th Battalion	—	22nd Battalion	—	27th Battalion
19th Battalion	—	24th Battalion *	—	28th Battalion
20th Battalion	—	25th Battalion	—	29th Battalion
21st Battalion	—	26th Battalion	—	31st Battalion

* NOTE: Leo served in the 24th Battalion

CHAPTER 4

Montreal and Leo's Departure for England

L eo was young and enthusiastic and he wanted to go to war. Later, as conscription loomed, he recounts in a letter that he was glad he enlisted early, because there really was no practical alternative.

Leo's letters from Montreal indicate a good humoured, fun-loving young man focused on having a good time. A private in the army, but a Loyola college graduate with friends to play with, and money to support himself, Leo was able to attend social affairs, dances and watering places not normally frequented by "other ranks."

⁖

Montreal
May 2ⁿᵈ, 1915

Dear Gertie:

> *I have had such a gay week of it that I just couldn't possibly get a moment to scribble a letter home. Monday night a bunch of us went out to movie show had a feed at Brysons and got in around twelve, Tuesday night Joe and his friend Miss Keene and I went down to the Jardin and had a peach night and on my way up met Joe so he telephoned Marie's friend and the four of us went down to the Imperial and ended up at the Jardin, we had fun dances and came home as we had to be in barracks before twelve.*

> *Friday went to the Cookes and danced once more but I got away early on an excuse that I had to be in barracks.*

> *Saturday aft. had a half holiday so Inez and I and Joe and his friend went down to the Windsor if you please,*

had tea and danced till 6.15 oh some class, they have a swell orchestra, but the floor is so crowded a good thing they are not dancing the old waltz or I am afraid my runs down the floor which I used to do at home wouldn't go very far.

I love the new dances now and do enjoy dancing to an orchestra; it is a little different than Joe Davis's old Victrola last summer. Saturday night Joe and I were to meet Somers in the writing room at the Windsor at 8 but we got a telephone message to come down to the St Regis so we met him there and went to a movie show got out at 10 and had no place to go, so of course made for the Jardin again.

We didn't bring partners this time so made up our minds we had to get them there. We spoke to different fellows and got them to introduce us to any girls they knew and I had the time of my life had about 14 dances.

I was dancing with one queen, when she said ah! There is Robertson, don't you know him, I looked around and there was one of our old officers and Major Parr, that was goodbye to my little queen after that dance I left her where I found her and old Parr walked up and had the next dance, he sat there the rest of the evening and I hadn't the nerve to walk up and take my major's young lady for another dance (hard luck being a private) but we had a big joke over it anyway.

I had a pass to go out to Zadie's today but hadn't any money, that's for having too good a time, so I went up to Charlie's and had a sleep and here I am writing this.

I think Joe and I will take our friends to the Jardin on Tuesday night again, if we can see our way through our pockets Oh! What's the diff. we might as well have a good time now, as in a few weeks it will be all over, and it is a better way, to spend your money than blowing it in a bar room like the rest of the crowd do.

I wonder if I could teach you the fox trot in this letter, the one they are doing now in New York and here, which is demonstrated at the Jardin by a couple from N.Y.

The lady going backwards 8 long steps with about two beats to each step, then after you have done the eight, 4 two steps starting on the left side take one two step making a sort of half turn to the left, then the same thing back again making a half turn to the right you do this twice making four steps in all, that brings you back again to where you were when you finished the 8 long steps, keep on moving taking 4 glides to the left and sort of half turn to the right and take 4 glides back again the start off with 4 long steps starting with the left foot the same as the 8 steps at the beginning, the stop with the gentleman having his left foot forward as if stopped in the middle of a step and do sort of sway backwards and forwards, which is called the balance do this balance 4 times and the start off on the 8 long steps again and do the same thing over, now if you read this over carefully and copy it out so you can read it, I think you will pick up the fox trot in one evening.

I know Inez and I watched them one evening at the Jardin when it was shown for the first time. We remembered it and had a practice another night before we came down and danced it at the Jardin and got on fine. Now they are only dancing that fox trot everywhere you never see the old one that I was trying to show you when I was down.

I have so many letters to write I don't know what I am going to do. What has Mama decided to do about Mtl., never a word since she first said something about it? I am in hopes of getting a letter tomorrow

Tell Stella Corinne will be going back to Quebec in a few days and then home again, she is now in Three Rivers. Chas. has shaved his mustache off this a.m.

Bye Bye — love to you all

Your old soldier

Leo

ঙ

Leo's battalion sailed on Monday, May 11th, 1915 and arrived in England May 20th. Five days after his arrival he was admitted to Moore Barracks General Hospital in Shorncliffe having contracted spinal meningitis. He was discharged on Monday July 5th.

ঙ

S.S. Cameronia

Wednesday, May 13th, 1915

8:10 PM

Dear Mamma:

> *We are now about 50 miles off Cape Gaspé and heading South East, dear knows where we are going on that course but I should worry, as long as we turn up some where, I was awfully disappointed not to turn into Gaspé Bay, as I fully expected we would wait for the other boats there or that the boats which have already left Montreal would be waiting for us. But we passed right on, I could see the Cape quite plainly and also Perce Mountains, we could see Anticosti on the Port side also I think I will try and give you a description of our departure & voyage so far and will keep it up everyday until I can mail this.*

> *Monday (May 11th) reveille sounded at 4:30 the last notes were not finished before the Barracks was in a howl, every body began yelling & singing & kept it up till breakfast after we had something to eat I guess we all felt better & still made more noise, the morning was spent packing, we were confined to barracks all day, so couldn't get out. In the aft. we sat in the windows of our rooms & called out to everybody & sang songs, 7:15 the people began to gather on Peel*

St. at Metcalfe, I made out Charlie in the crowd & he managed to get a letter in to me, but not from home which I expected. 8:45 we marched out in the street in platoons together & were cheered and clapped over & over again, the Police soon lost control of the crowd & we had an awful time they crowded around us like flies & when we got the order to form fours and march off we couldn't get into fours, my it was some send off, & most likely you will not see a word of it in the papers.

We marched down Metcalfe Street & when we got to St. Catherine we couldn't push our way through we marched in fours, two abreast & single file, people crowded into the ranks & walked with us everybody cheering clapping & shaking your hand & wishing you good luck, well they all went mad that's all, girls would throw their arms around you & kiss you good bye, never having seen you before cry all over you & wish you good luck, we pushed our way down St. Catherine Street having an awful time of it, men would walk along side and beg to carry your kit for you, saying you will have to carry it far enough before you get back after shaking hands with at least 3 thousand people we arrived at St Lawrence Main St. & marched down, when we arrived down near the docks the crowd I think was still greater, every pretty girl I would hold out my hand to & say good bye as if we had been old pals, they would take your arm & walk along a way till they got jammed up in the crowd & left behind. I saw some girls I knew & boys who went to Loyola also Douglas Annett & the family, but any amount of others who I know were down I never saw, you know you could only make out the ones on the inside when we arrived at the dock we marched in one by one & left the crowd cheering and waving flap hats handkerchiefs & what ever they had, one girl wanted me to take her ring & wear it, but I wouldn't take it.

Well we left the crowd and marched aboard, we were with some of the first so were put into the worst quarters first & certainly got rotten quarters away up in the bow and down under the water nearly, God help us if we have any heavy weather. But the meals are very good, much better than in Barracks.

We wandered around the ship that night before going to bed; it was then late as it took nearly an hour and a half to make it through that awful crowd. Everybody says they never heard of such a send off & such a crowd before or ever expects to see it again.

We left Montreal at 5:30 I awoke but was too tired to get up so went to sleep & awoke at 7 had breakfast and went on deck, every ship we met they saluted & cheered us & we answered with three blasts, passed through Three Rivers about 10 AM (May 12th) every ship at the wharves & every mill & factory in the town tooted their horns, there was a big bunch waving from all over the town. Most of our morning was spent in answering salutes & yelling our heads off. Called at Quebec at 3 o'clock & took on 90 men from Bermuda going to the front & some officers, saw the old Cascapedia & Lady Gaspé there, but they seemed dead nobody about. There were not many on the wharf, I wish I could have seen Esther or some of the Grogans, we left again a little after four & passed a good many ships on the way, went to bed at 9 and was up at 6:30 (May 13th) found we were pretty well down river it is a little different on a boat like this than on one of ours, we are running between 16 & 18 knots all the time & last night I think they even did better. Today we had boat drill & all turned out with our life belts on, but didn't do much.

About 9 am we ran into a school of whales they were spouting all around us, one big fish followed us for about a half hour only 25 feet from the boat I don't know what it was it acted like a porpoise but was black & had a fin on it's back I thought it was a porpoise. I thought porpoises were white.

5 PM found us off Gaspé, but kept straight out for a few hours & now have changed our course to the South.

I am writing this down in the dining room we are beginning to feel a bit of a roll now but nothing to speak of, it has been beautiful weather so far but I am afraid we are in for rain before too long.

What a change to see the hills along Gaspé with straw on them yet the boys couldn't make it out at all, and many were surprised when they heard I came from that God forbidden coast, but still they admired it and thought it beautiful.

It is awfully funny to stand around and listen to the different conversations, some will be saying that is Newfoundland over there, others no it's Anticosti and it was all the time the North coast of the St. Lawrence. I nearly had one fellow put up a $10 spot that we were off the coast of Cape Breton & we were just off Fame Point all the time, by the rate we were going we would be in England by tomorrow.

Well good night & I will try & write a few lines tomorrow again, I wish you could put all my letters away from now on, I would like to see them when I come back, I haven't time to write a diary, so this will be just as good.

Saturday 7 PM (May 16ᵗʰ)

This has been at a stand still the last three days. I have been sick, my God talk about sick. Thursday I thought I would write after supper but a strong westerly wind came up & this tub just about empty rolled around like a nut shell talk about roll, pitch & stand on end all the same time. I wasn't sick Thursday (May 14ᵗʰ) night but wasn't in a writing humour but after having to sleep in the steerage stinking dirty hall I wasn't in a very good condi-

*tion in the morning anyway I came up on deck &
nearly turned wrong side out. I slept on the deck
all day nearly everybody in the same condition I
was, crawled down to my bunk at about 8 PM & fell
asleep, it's certainly traveling under difficulties taking a trip like this, but I suppose it's all in the game, I
got up on deck today & our company are eating in the
second class dining room so I made one good meal.
We are getting the dirty end of it alright this trip
having to travel steerage & eat there for the first five
days; anyway thank God we will have a respectable
place to eat in anyway after this. But I will be glad
when the trip is over.*

*After leaving Cape Gaspé we traveled just
about south till yesterday morning when we changed
our course to Southeast & last night sometime
changed again to east, we must be away south of the
N.Y. route, as it is nice and warm and we are around
without coats all day. Today I got up in a hurry &
came up on deck have been feeling much better but
not well yet & there is such a roll tonight.*

*We have had a few boat drills the whistle
blows one long blast & we have to run for our life
belts & fall in, by our boat, have regular parade twice
a day do a little telegraph work & are issued with
another little bit of our equipment, it will be complete
in time I suppose. Our hours are reveille 6 AM, breakfast 7:45, parade 10:45, dinner 12, parade 2, supper
5. Go to bed or last post at 9:30 lights out 10.*

*We haven't seen a boat for days isn't it funny
we haven't a convoy yet, if a submarine should appear they would have us in ten minutes. Today has
been raining most of the time & yesterday foggy all
day. I hope the sun appears tomorrow for a change &
cheers everybody up.*

*Tuesday (May 19ᵗʰ) 1:30 PM here I have
slipped two days again, Sunday I was too lazy*

*to write & the weather foggy & raining as usual.
Saturday night I decided I would not go down to that
hole so we slept on deck. They washed the deck at 1
AM & I awoke all wet and had to crawl down to the
steerage and make the best of it. Sunday we had boat
drill & I slept on deck again till 1 AM & awoke as
usual all wet. Monday was seasick again and nearly
died lay around deck all day in the rain. I was bound
I wouldn't go down to that bunk, what a shame to put
men in such a place the smell is enough to kill anyone. I would like to give some of these officers a piece
of my mind, you know they could easily find place for
us in the first class, but it would not just look well
to have privates in their quarters, damn them anyway. One of the fellows of no. 5 platoon took me in
his stateroom for the night & I had a good rest on the
floor. Today I am quite well and feeling fit & it is a
beautiful day & not very rough.*

*I believe we are to make a rush for it tomorrow
night, no convoy we rec'd orders today that every body
must remain on deck till the ship lands. We must all
have our life belts on & must keep our heads below
the rail, we also will have all lights out & God knows
what all. I think they are forgetting they have 1,800
men on board & also Sir Allan, I hope we make it
alright; we have four machine guns mounted on the
deck to shoot at the periscopes of the submarines. I
hope they do good but it sounds not to me.*

Wednesday (May 20th) 10:30 AM.

*We are all on deck with life belts on & hidden
below the rail. Here we have to stay until we reach
port, some joke! All the watertight doors are closed &
the boats lowered ready to jump into. We have no convoy yet, I don't suppose we will have one now.*

*I slept on deck last night & had a swell break-
fast this AM, was the last man to leave the table.*

The next time I go from Canada to Eng. believe me it won't be steerage or I will stay at home. I hope this letter won't smell of the place down there or I am sure you all will be seasick before you have read it.

We must be getting near land as there are a lot of birds around this morning, they have called for volunteer firemen & are going to push the old Cameronia 25 knots if we are chased they say she has been chased three times already and always managed to get away.

3:30 PM two torpedo boat destroyers have just caught up to us all are steaming alongside, I tell you it makes you feel a bit safer, they were certainly welcomed by everyone, I guess we will now run straight into port God knows what port or even where we are.

You should see the little destroyer steaming along with us as if she was king of the seas; there is some class to the Navy alright. We were going through the fog turning and twisting in every direction then suddenly this little terrier appears on the horizon & catches up to us.

Goodbye Mamma dear will write you again as soon as we land. They are around for the mail.

Love and kisses to all, your boy Leo

Military Hospital
Shorncliffe
June 3rd, 1915

Dear Mum:
I have again gone and given you a whole lot of trouble & worry, I was so put out when I found I had to go to the hospital because I know you all would worry yourselves half to death over me, but thank God I am nearly over it now and you more likely have been kept posted all along and now have a big cable

*bill to pay. I have been a very lucky boy and got off
with only a slight attack and I am making wonderful
progress and soon hope to be up again new.*

*Sunday night I felt out of sorts and went to
bed thinking I had a bad attack of grippe and was
awfully sick all night. Monday I got up and paraded
sick before the doctor and he put me to bed where I remained with a splitting headache till Tuesday when
I was taken off to Shorncliffe Canadian Military
Hospital, the Canadian nurses were very good to me,
I had one for the day and another for night and room
to myself and God only knows what I suffered all I
can remember is the dreadful headache and when
they would inject some dope in my arm to put me to
sleep.*

*Friday I was moved down to the English
hospital & put in a ward, I was so sorry to leave my
nurses they had been so kind but the doctor said I
had to go and so I just had to but I was better then
and not suffering anymore and have been improving
ever since.*

*They are all very kind down here have a day
and night nurse and the ward they have young men
doing all the work who are all very good.*

*The treatment in this disease is to tap you
they punch a hole in the small of your back and draw
the water or whatever it is off your spine and it's this
stuff on your brain that gives the dreadful headache.*

*I was awfully surprised to see Alma at the
door one day, I was over the worst of it, but she could
not come in the ward to see me, I suppose she has
written to tell you all about it. I also had a letter from
her yesterday.*

*Perhaps I will go down and spend a few days
with her in London as soon as I get out, she told me
to try and she would be able to look after me, I hope
they let me out soon.*

*I see a lot of Canadian officers they all come
in and ask how the Canadian is, one fellow seemed to*

*know the family. Turner of Que., he asked about my
uncle who used to be at Thunder River. He also says
Bertram Faunell is with them, (the McGill Hospital)
did Papa know that?*

*I had a letter today from one of the fellows at
camp & he says when I was taken to hospital they
were all quarantined & haven't left camp yet, the
poor chap that very day his father and mother came
to Folkstone and have been there since and he hasn't
seen them.*

*I have had only one letter from you & that was
one written to Montreal, forwarded by Chas. I wonder
where my mail is, that's all the news. I have had from
Canada except a cable from Chas.*

*How did you hear I was sick anyway was it
published in the papers?*

*Bye bye mum, dear this is too hard work just
yet.*

*Don't worry now as I am quite all right again
and will soon be about.*

*Your loving boy,
Leo*

Military Hospital, Shorncliffe

June 6ᵗʰ, 1915

Dear Mom:

*Well I have been two weeks in bed today.
SOME SOLDIER. And I wonder how much longer I
will be before I am on my feet and about again?*

*I am feeling quite well now, only a bit sick and
a dare say it will be some time before I am quite myself, but let's hope for the best.*

*There is one thing I can do and that is eat, in
the morning I have a big cup of milk, two big pieces of
bread and butter and an egg. Dinner a whole chicken,*

*boiled potatoes and a mug of chicken broth, milk and
pudding, then at four thirty they have tea as they call
it – bread and butter and milk and at seven supper
which is a big mug of cocoa. Not too bad for a person
who is supposed to be in bed sick, is it?*

*Yesterday I got quite a surprise when Herbert
Pimm walked into the ward, he received a cable from
Charles telling him I was sick and came and looked
me up. The poor fellow didn't know my number or
regiment and had an awful time to find me and after two hours he at last came to find the Canadian
Hospital and they told him there where I was moved
to, they let him in to see me but only could stay for
only a few minutes so he came back again at about
five o'clock and remained with me until nearly six,
then took the seven o'clock train back to London. An
awfully nice chap he seemed to me, and very kind.
He says if I will just drop him a card when I can get
leave and he will meet me at the station and take me
all over London as he did you and Papa last winter.*

*I haven't had a letter yet from you except the
first one. I wonder what you are all doing just now
suppose getting ready for Church as we are five hours
ahead and it's now two o'clock. I suppose by now
there is no sign of snow and you are enjoying a Gaspé
summer day. How beautiful it must be, my first summer away isn't it?*

*How has Bert done with his farm this year, is
he working very hard and did he break any new land,
how is Trixie and all the animals. Trixie must look
awfully nice with her summer coat. Tell Bert he must
write and give me all the news and about the boat,
is she working well this year and does Bert use her
much.*

*Well I wonder this old war is going to last,
they are advertising for three hundred thousand more
men and I guess they want them badly the way they
are working to make men enlist, the papers are full
of nothing else knocking those who won't offer their*

*services, they want every man who's fit in uniform. I
wonder how the Canadians are coming forward now?
I haven't any news in this old place so Bye Bye Moms
dear, love and kisses to all.*

Your boy Leo

*(Don't worry now dear as I am all over it. Just have
to hang around and get strong. Now and then I am
going to London for a week if I can get away.)*

Military Hospital

Shorncliffe

June 8th, 1915

Dear Zadie:

*Some soldier you must be thinking me, but
never mind it can't be helped and there is no one as
angry at me as I am with myself. Here I am lying in
bed like a damn child absolutely useless. And what a
time I have had damn near died you know two weeks
and two days in bed today and still no signs of getting up for weeks yet. I have done wonderfully tho.
And am feeling quite well only a bit weak.*

*Well Zadie I had just started a letter to you
and was writing on a Sunday afternoon when I felt
tired and fell off to sleep. I awoke with a headache
and went to my bunk for a rest where I never got. I
don't know what has become of what I did write.*

*I was then taken up to the Canadian hospi-
tal first where I had a room and two nurses but as
soon as I was a bit better they moved me down to the
English hospital. I was sorry to have to leave but had
to go so that's all about it.*

*I have been treated very well here too every one
is very kind.*

Alma came up from London about a week ago but they wouldn't let her in to see me, I just saw her thro the window and last Saturday Herbert Pimm walked into the ward. My, was I surprised to see him. Chas. Cabled him he said. I think he was so kind to come away up here and lose a whole day over me. He had a hard time finding me, and then they told him he could stay only a little while. So he came in again at about five and remained till nearly half past six and took the 7 o'clock train back to London. He is awfully kind I think and wants me to let him know when I go to London and he is going to meet me and show me the village I couldn't make out who he was at first but after I could see how much he looked like Chas. his way is very much the same. Tell Bob his brother is a damn decent chap I think. He spoke a lot of Bob and wanted to know how he was getting on.

Well what I have seen of England I think is beautiful we had a nice run from Plymouth up on the train and have been down to Hythe and took a bus to Folkestone one day and came back to Sandling by train. That's all I have seen yet of the country I hope to get to London some day. My bed is just by the window here and when I sit up I can see out on the English channel and on a clear day can see France I believe we are only about 35 miles from the firing line

Alma says the Clarkes are living at Oxford she spent a few days with them, he is with the O.T.C. whatever that might be.

Alma sent me a postal wanting to know if I wanted fruit or anything in the way of eats.

I suppose Lauretta will have left you when this reaches you, mails take such a long time to get anywhere it seems. What do you intend doing this summer? Going down to dear old Gaspé or remaining in Alexandria.

Well bye bye dear will try to write soon again.

Your old bro.

Leo

(Ps. How is Bob, tell him to be good.)

ಐ

Leo is recovering in Hospital from his bout with cerebral spinal meningitis. The Hospital is R.A.M.C. Hospital Shorncliffe, located near Folkstone England near Dover. Leo comments that he could see the "white cliffs" of France from the lawn of the hospital.

ಐ

R.A.M.C Hospital

June 13th, 1915

Dear Papa:
　　You will see by the heading that I am still an invalid, but am doing very well, I am writing this sitting in a big chair out of doors this is my second day out, yesterday I came out at about three o'clock & remained out till six & today I got up just before dinner & am now settled down for a good afternoon in the sun & fresh air.
　　It is really beautiful here & I wish I was strong enough to wander around, but my distance for walking is very limited, as I find I have all I can do to get from my ward out here, that is only about fifteen yds.
　　The hospital is situated on a hill overlooking the water & today I can see the white cliffs of France quite easily, the water is just dotted with boats going up and down you would never think there was a war going on, & when you think of the thousands of boats going in and out of ports daily you know the Germans are really doing nothing with their submarines what

is one boat every now and again when you consider the numbers that are moving about.

I haven't received any news from home since I last wrote; I guess I am just about to give up expecting any more. I think if I can arrange it I am going to London & remain with Alma for ten days or so till I get strong, she said for me to come & stay with her as soon as I was strong enough to get out of the hospital so if they will let me go there instead of to a convalescent home I would like it much better, but I will have to get my doctor to recommend me for ten days leave or so & that will be the hardest part.

I suppose you will have Lauretta home very soon & is Zadie coming down this summer, it would be nice to have them both home again. How is everybody and are you kept very busy.

What is the St. Maurice doing & have the Chandler people made any difference in the work having their stuff shipped & rcd. by Sandy beach.

Hoping to hear soon from you.

Your loving son,
Leo.

Military Hospital, Shorncliffe

June 20ᵗʰ, 1915

Dear Mamma:

I have made wonderful progress since my last letter to you and am now walking about quite easily. I get up in the morning about 8:30 after having my breakfast in bed, wash shave and get all dolled up in my blue hospital uniform with a big red tie, then I wash up the dishes, sweep out my ward, and push my big chair out of doors in the sun and read all day. I think this week tho will see my visit here at an end.

Had a long letter from Joe yesterday, they are out of quarantine and doing a lot of target shooting. He says they get up at 4:30 have breakfast and are ready to leave Camp at 5:30, they then march down to Hythe arriving there at 6:30 and shoot all day 200 & 300 ranges so far, both slow and rapid shooting. I am sorry to be missing that.

The sister took my picture the other day and it turned out pretty well except that my hair is so long (not having a haircut since I left Canada). I was telling sister you will never say I was sick when you see it. I am sitting up in a chair with my beach face as if I owned the place. I have got awfully burned again since I have been sitting in the sun and this sea air is worse than Gaspé.

I have been talking to a lot of wounded soldiers lately and have a good idea of the front as far as danger and hardships go. A bunch of Canadian soldiers were passing and noticed my Canadian boots so came over to talk to me. They were all wounded at Ypres they said it was mighty hot for a while most of them are drilled thro. the leg or arm. We have one fellow in my division an English regular who was in the retreat from Mons he was shot thro the hand a very young chap, then we see a lot of poor fellows minus a leg or arm hopping about, all quite cheerful.

I was awfully sorry to hear of poor Dr. Wakeham's death, it's too sad the poor old fellow, I am afraid he'll be very much missed won't he.

I received the Standard yesterday. I wonder who has subscribed to it for me as it was mailed from the office and has no stamps on it.

It is an awful difference reading an English paper then a Canadian one about the War news. The English papers hardly say anything or just a few out lines, very often they just say "there is nothing to report today", but the Canadians do seem to make a lot of reading matter don't they.

I am glad Gaspé is sending a few men now 15 in the last lot that is really fine, I only wish they had come along with me, it would be nice to have a few fellows from your home with you wouldn't it?

I don't know if Mich would get through, is he still talking of a commission? His eyes might not bother him if he goes as an officer as I see a lot of them with glasses.

I have received all your letters so far Stella's being the last numbered #2 that is a good idea to number them. I expect to hear from you tomorrow.

Good bye mum dear don't worry any more as I am through with the hard luck things are going to be all my way now.

Love and kisses to all not forgetting your own dear self.

Your loving Leo.

Military Hospital

Shorncliffe

Sunday, June 27ᵗʰ, 1915

Dear Mom:

Rcd. your letter the day before yesterday but as there is no Canadian mail until the 30ᵗʰ I waited until today to write.

You poor people, how worried you have been, I knew when I was taken sick it would worry you all to death and I guess that's all I talked about when I was bad.

But thanks to all your prayers that I recovered so quickly, as you know I was two weeks and a half in bed. And here the other poor chap who came in only a few days after me is still helpless and hardly knows what's going on yet and they say I was much worse than he in the beginning.

I have no fear of the Front at all as long as I have all your pious prayers, for I know they will all be heard.

I hadn't any mail for two weeks when I received your letter and with it came eight other letters and four papers. I had the best evening I have had for a long time reading all the news.

I had a letter from Mrs. Amy with a stamped and addressed envelope for me to write and let her know how I am getting on and if she could send me a Jersey cake and tobacco. Awfully good of her don't you think? Of course I answered the same day.

I am perfectly well now. I run about and play all day with the orderlies or sit out on the bank and wave to the girls passing on the street. But they are keeping me here because they say I may still have the germs on my throat and could give it to anybody.

My Officer came up to see me the other night. He said he came up to see me often but they wouldn't let him in, he would like very much to have me back in a week from Wednesday as they are taking up a lot of new work.

Well things are looking up a bit better for the Allies, I hope it keeps up; although Lemberg has fallen they are not going to gain anything by it. France and Italy are having a succession of victories the Australians are doing wonderful work. We never hear very much of the British as they don't publish a great deal but they are holding their own. I suppose you heard of Flight. Lieut. Warnford. It's awfully sad he should lose his life after all that. By the way did you cut out the story of our departure, if you did would you please send it to me, I will return it again as I hear from everybody even Mrs. Amy they saw our wonderful send off in the Star and I would like to see it.

*I wonder who is sending me the Standard;
I am so pleased to get a Canadian paper. I read it
through and through.*

*Had a letter from Mrs. Frances, Mick's sister
inquiring about me. They want me to go down to
Bromley as soon as I am well enough which I am going to try and do, I answered her and thanked them
for being so kind.*

*I am enclosing a few snaps one of the sisters
took, the one of the two nurses and four boys are the
staff of "E" Division, they are all very kind and the
boys good fun, they all tease me about Canada and
the expression I use, especially "sure", "right here"
and a few others that sleepy Eng. never heard from.
But I stand up for old Canada and don't forget to re-
mind them of their weak points that are numerous.*

*How is everything at home, tell Bert to write
and give me all the news of the farm and etc. and etc.*

*I hear you are not having a regatta this year,
but tell Lauretta for next year as we are going to win
that mixed tandem.*

*With love to all and hoping to hear from you
all your loving son Lills.*

Military Hospital, Shorncliffe

July 3ʳᵈ, 1915

Dear Stella;\:

*I received your letters of the 10ᵗʰ & 16ᵗʰ &
also Mamma's of the 14ᵗʰ the last two came together
tonight. I am so glad & happy to know you have my
letter & the one the nurse wrote. I was always won-
dering if she wrote as she said she would & took your
address as they were taking me away to the RAMC
Hospital. My those nurses were kind to me I wish
I could see them again but, there is so much damn*

*red tape about this military life as you know & they
hold the rank of lieut. & of course could not be seen
mixing with privates. Well I will never forget those
two nurses; you said the one that wrote was Miss.
Andrews. I don't know what the other one's name
was, and this is the first time I knew this one, I was
too sick when I was up there to bother about names,
and as soon as my head was a bit better they moved
me down here. And since I have been up and running about you know I have had a great time, and
the last week has been a continual roughhouse. We
are only two patients now and the other chap is still
in bed, so I play all day with the orderlies. I spent the
afternoon rolling down the hill with one chap, it's really wonderful how I am getting my strength back,
I am almost as strong as ever I was, I was one too
many for this chap anyway and nearly always managed to knock him end over end over the hill. We had
a great laugh once he had me going backward to the
edge of the hill at a quick rate. So I thought I would
try Tommy Fitzpatrick's trick and waited till I got to
the edge and threw myself on my back and let him
go over my head. The hill was so steep that he never
hit till he was at the bottom and then fell on his head
and nearly killed him.*

*Well Tells, I am leaving here Monday and
going to London for a week and then back to work.
I have written to Alma and she is to meet me at
Charing Cross.*

*You know I have had such a good time I am
now sorry to leave, been so comfortable and good
meals and a good hospital staff, the boys used to
take me up to their tent every now and then and we
would have musical evening, something like Lewis
and I used to have in the kitchen last winter. I have
had letters from Mrs. Amy asking how much money I
would need but I haven't answered yet as I am going
to wait till I get paid Monday at my regiment, and
if they don't stop any of my pay, I will be able to see*

me through, if they do I will ask for some. At present I haven't a damn cent and am writing with my last stamp, they took all the money I had in my pocket and sent it to the regiment only keeping two shillings that I have spent on stamps.

The mail from Jersey takes nearly as long to come as from Canada.

I will be rich six weeks Sunday the time I lost signaling, I will have to do some work to catch up now, but I think I can manage. We have now nine motorcycles and nine bicycles for the signalers, you will see me speeding around England some morning before breakfast.

And you have had a lot of inquiries about me from my friends, I tell you the friends you have in Gaspé and on the coast are worth having aren't they.

Tells my next letter will be from London, I will see Herbert Pimm and Mrs. Francis, I had a letter from the latter & she says her mother is in an awful way over Mich enlisting.

Write often love and kisses to all.
Leo

183 Cromwell Rd.

London S.W.

July 12ᵗʰ, 1915

Dear Papa:

It is some time since I have written but I thought Alma Kavanaugh would do for a few days & then I sent a cable when I arrived in London.

I have all your letters I think the last being Gertie's written on the 18ᵗʰ, Mamas on the 20ᵗʰ & yours on the 22ⁿᵈ. I have been here a week now & am enjoying myself, you would not think I had ever been sick, I can walk the whole day and never even get tired. Monday I got my discharge

*from hospital & took the train to Sandling I got off there
& got my money & caught the 5:09 for London. Arrived in
London at 7:30 Alma met me at Charing Cross & we went
to Regent palace and had dinner afterwards walked to Hyde
Park & listened to the band for an hour or so and took a
bus home. Home is a very nice little room in Kensington
with good meals more of a home than a boarding house &
only 5/ a day. Tuesday we took the tube down to Piccadilly
& then walked about and saw all the sights in the aft. Had
afternoon tea at some joint & danced. In the evening went
to the Hippodrome. Wednesday did a little shopping in the
morning & went to Mme Toussauds in the aft. Geoffrey came
into town for the evening & the three of us went down to
Piccadilly & walked about, had supper about eleven & came
home. Thursday Alma left me, she has gone into the Chelsea
Hospital nursing, so I started off alone in the morning and
took the tube, went to see the Horse Guards & walked down
to the Parliament buildings up Regent Street & came home
& called up Herbert Pimm & met him at 2:30 at Charing
Cross, we then went to the Guild Hall & St. Paul had tea &
went down to his factory. I met Alma in the evening and we
went for a little walk. Friday had lunch with Pimm & went
through the Tower, lunch at Cheshire Cheese, saw the Bank
of England Royal Exchange, Mansion House, went down to
call Alma in the evening & we went for a bus ride to Autsrey.
Next day Alma was off in the morning so we went down to
the city & fooled about, saw Admiralty Offices, Waterloo
& had lunch. Went through at James Park & then through
Westminster Abbey, Caught the 4:08 to Twickingham & spent
the week end with them, he has a very nice little house &
wife. They were so kind & everything so much like home.
Sunday we went on to Windsor, saw the castle it is beautiful
you didn't go out to Windsor did you? Came back with Pimm
this AM on the 8:30 & here I am. I think we will go out to the
Zoo this aft.*

*I have not written to Mrs. Amy for money as I have
enough to see me through. I think you are far too kind Papa,
I wish I knew where Millin was I could go and see him, I
hope it is not a serious wound.*

*Mamma talks of my going home to get strong again
but I guess by now you will know there isn't any need of it
as I am my old self again, feel just as strong as I ever did &
with a week or two in the regiment again I will be fit for anything.*

*My regimental officer called me in his office the day
I came back & told me if anybody would come back from the
front I would, as I am the luckiest man there ever was. Alma
tells me I should be crazy but she has been watching me for
days & I am quite alright. I think I am a lucky boy. Things
were a bit better at the front these last...With much love to all
& hoping you are all well and having a good summer.*

Your loving son,

Leo.

*P.S. ever see such a place as London to find your
way about, it is beautifully laid out, the streets seem to run
into one another & there is not a straight street in the whole
place then they have these circuses with streets going in every direction.*

Sandling

July 20ᵗʰ, 1915

Dear Zadie:

*I haven't written to you for some time and I
expect you hear from home how I am getting on.*

*Well to start off with I am back at work, got
out of hospital on the 5ᵗʰ and went to London for ten
days, I was with Alma for three days then she went
into the Chelsea Hospital (Fulham Rd. SW London)
nursing, so I called up Herbert Pimm and he carted
me all over London, we saw all the principal sights
I guess and how I did enjoy it. Nearly every morning
we would have lunch together and then start out. I*

*think I took up a lot of his valuable time as he took
over half a day with me every day I was in London,
then I went out to his home for the weekend and on
to Windsor Sunday passed thro Staines, he pointed
out where the old home was and told me some of the
funny things Bob and they did, what dreadful boys.*

*Tell Bob I met Mr. Carr who is married to
Chas' wife's sister.*

*I have so much to tell you I haven't any idea
how to start and Zadie I have heaps of letters to answer, I never wrote while I was in London and everybody seems to have taken pity on me and written so
I will just tell you I have had a hell of a good time in
London graced around all day and went to shows at
night also went to Richmond. I found it quite hard to
get around at first and used to sport about in a Taxi
most of the time but at the end of my ten days leave I
could get anywhere I liked with the help of a bus or
underground, some London and with the Canadian
uniform you really could have a real good time.*

*Came back to camp Thursday 15th. I haven't
been doing very much, everybody is awfully kind to
me and I haven't had to go out on marches unless I
like to and I don't do any hard work out in the field
laying telephone cable and if I went asleep they never
awoke me until they were ready to march back to
camp. Tomorrow we are going out for three days I
don't know if they will let me go or not.*

*We are doing very little flag work I under-
stand only field telephone is used in the field and a
bit of semaphore, I have a lot of back work to get up
and have some practicing to do on that and buzzer
as they have picked up a bit of speed and I have been
absent for over two months but I think it will all come
in time*

*Saturday I went down to Folkestone with one
of the boys and we went to the hotel and had a damn*

good meal Monday night I went down again and we went to the theatre and the walked around and got in at 12.30 when we should have been in bed at ten. But I am always lucky in getting past the guard.

You must miss Gaspé and you won't be going down this summer well lets hope we will all be home together next summer won't it be grand.

Give my love to all the Alexandria...and remember me to Bob tell him he has a very kind brother and reminds me of him very much, Write again often Zadie dear.

With much love,

Leo

Sandling

July 28ᵗʰ, 1915

Dear Lauretta:

Received your letter, Stella's and one from Bert last night and also the Standard and two graphics, some mail but all welcome.

I was glad to hear you had received my cable I sent in London. I had a great laugh over Stella's letter and beautiful Jessie the girl is a fool, too bad the whole family are inclined that way and your friend Ernest is doing nothing in Gaspé can't they send him to Montreal and make him enlist, it's too bad we have to fight for those "good for nothings".

Who writes to the Campbellton Graphic, poor Charlie had his name in the paper for fair this time and also Marion and Stella, they must have had a most delightful trip to the Southwest.

And the salmon fishing is good this year just because I am not home; remember our excursion last year and all the fish we caught?

Last Sunday I went up to St. Martin's place and found LeGrand then we all looked up Herbert Adams and Eric Eden, I didn't see Sandy Beattie. We had a long talk and I have arranged to take the bunch of them down to Folkstone Saturday, they are all looking very well and I think it will do those fellows so much good.

Went to Folkstone Sunday night and couldn't get a bus home so took a taxi with an Officer as far as Hythe and walked up to Sandling. Last night we were down again and saw the Quaker Girl, it was very good.

Have been working very hard this week, went out Monday and did trench work until about five p.m. and then marched home had supper and marched off again and did not get back to home till about two thirty We had the morning off but had to up at five thirty so I took my blanket out on the hill and had a good sleep. We were on duty all afternoon, today we left camp at nine and only got back after five, I am told we have a twenty two hour march starting tomorrow morning. I don't mind it a bit and am feeling awfully well, I haven't even sore feet and the fellows who have been at it ever since were came over here are limping around on these marches. We have to carry all our equipment which consists of your greatcoat, mess tin with one meal, hold all, housewife, pair of socks, in your pack then under your pack is fastened your blanket rolled up in your rubber sheet. On your belt is fastened your haversack and your bayonet, your water bottle holding about a quart hangs from your neck. Also fastened to your belt are two cartridge pouches holding a hundred and fifty rounds, then your rifle and a flag and very often a field telephone weighing nine pounds and a roll of wire. Some load, but you know you get used to having this on your back from morning till night that you don't hardly notice it. I will be in good trim for moose hunting when I get back.

I hope Bert had a good holiday with his friend, give her my love if she is there when this arrives and tell her I am going to write to her soon.

And there are two nice girls at Bakers Hotel I wish I was there just my luck to be away the summer all the nice girls are there, never mind they are easy to get here.

I received the little snap Stell left also some the other day which were very good. Poor Charlie leaning over the boat.

We will say good night as I want to get a good rest tonight as we have a hard day and most likely will not get sleep for twenty four hours after tonight.

Love to all,
Leo

Sandling Camp

Aug. 9th, 1915

Mrs. Amy sent me another cake yesterday.

Dear Lauretta:

I haven't received any letters from home since I last wrote, but will scribble a few lines anyway as we are off out for the night and don't know when I will be back.

We have had a very busy week of it, out day and night and with very little sleep and of course it has to rain everyday just to keep you wet all the time and uncomfortable. Last Sunday night we started out about 10:30 I think it was and got back sometime in the early morning. Slept all morning.

Tuesday we were out all day and also Wednesday, Thursday we were inspected by Hughes & Bonar Law, in the rain, I wonder if it was in the Canadian papers.

I just wish some of you people were over here to see your Canadian chaps. I tell you it's an honour to be one of them and better still to be one of the old 24ᵗʰ. We were about 40 thousand and to look down that field as we marched up to form in platoons for the march past, all the bayonets fixed and all in line, the steel just looked like a huge piece of ice, then we formed up in platoons and marched past, everyman in step every man perfectly in line and all the hands swinging together, each platoon containing 60 men looked like one man it took over an hour for them all to march past and everyone was perfect. Our Colonel told us as we started down the field "now boys when you get eyes right, make your eyeballs crack as you turn them right" and we nearly did. I believe we will be inspected by Kitchener and the King on the 14ᵗʰ, how I wish some of you were here to see it. You can be proud of Canada's army there is not a soldier like them in the world one of the wounded were telling me, in a bayonet charge when the order is given the boys all spring together and the first thing you see over the trench is a row of steel then the most awful yells and swears and curses at the enemy. The trouble with them is they are too quick and are always in the thick of it before the slow English get up. I think that's why their losses are so great. Went to London this weekend and took Alma to a show Saturday night, Sunday I slept in till twelve o'clock. The first rest I have had since I left the hospital. Sunday aft. Alma and I went out to Bromley and saw the Francis' she is awful nice I think. We had tea with them and had to rush back to London, as I had to leave on the 9 o'clock train.

I didn't walk at all in London, took a taxi everywhere and did enjoy myself. Got back at 12 PM and had to be in parade at 7 AM. We were out all day and just got in for supper at 6. And are off again for the night in a few minutes, it's wonderful how I am standing it. Seeing what I have just been thro, but I

*am feeling so well and Alma says am looking wonder-
ful.*

*Geofrey has gone to the front, left a week ago,
poor Alma is rather worried I think, but is quite
brave.*

*I went up to see Berchervaise the other night
he is quite well again now.*

*I got a very nice raincoat from Alma that
Geoffrey left behind him. It will suit me fine instead
of my heavy great coat.*

*God knows when we are going to the front;
we may be here a long time yet it looks as if they will
keep us for the winter fighting.*

Love to everybody and all write often.

Your loving bro.

Leo

Sandling

Sept. 10ᵗʰ, 1915

Dear Papa:

*I wrote you some time ago but I guess my let-
ter went down to the bottom of the sea. I have your
letter of the 19ᵗʰ and Lauretta's written a few days
earlier. I also received one from Zadie about the same
time. I am sorry I haven't time to write the people
Sam spoke about, as we leave for France in the morning, I am going with nine other signalers and the
transports also a few men of the Coy as the advance
guard, I suppose the Battalion will be coming over in
a few days. We were told this morning and are to be
ready for tomorrow but I suppose we won't go for a
few days as usual, they always keep you waiting days
after you really are supposed to go we are on bicycles
so most likely our work will be dispatch riding till the*

Bn. gets up to the trenches. I think we will sail from Southampton.

Tell Sams I visited the castle that he spoke of and we had our course of musketry at Hythe. I am sorry I haven't had the time to look up his people. Was he living anywhere in this district?

They are practicing bomb throwing about 75 yards from where I am and you should hear the noise when those things burst, of course there is no shrapnel in the cans so there is no danger unless it bursts very near you. But they do make a noise when about 6 explode one after the other.

The Zeppelins are doing a lot of damage again. They will have to destroy a few more of them. I was speaking to a wounded corporal from the front yesterday and he says just as soon as the allies can get enough munitions together they will drive the Germans back so fast they won't know where they are. He says they can drop 7 shells on every 20 square feet of ground and keep doing it as long as the ammunition holds out. They say it was done already as a test but in no time they hardly had any shells left. The artillery that day was one continual roar like a machine gun. Then they say when we charge the devils will put up their hands and say "Friends, friends", but the Canadians give them the bayonet that's the mercy they need.

I thought of making over about $15 or $20 dollars a month to you but I am advised not to do it now as I am going to the front and you might never receive the money or find out my agreement, so let it go to my account in the London Office and will draw it after the war or if I should be wounded I could get it then. Now if anything happens to me, I am paid up to Sept. 1ˢᵗ in full, from this time on, we will draw only 20 cents a day, so you be sure you get anything that's coming to me. I have worked damn hard for it and the Government won't have it.

I am feeling quite strong and well and ready for the fray. I dare say my last letter wasn't very cheerful but I was in a bad humour that night.

I got a nice Jersey Cake from Mrs. Amy today. She has been awfully kind to me. I was glad to hear they did so well with the bazaar, father Richard must have been pleased with $2,500.

Col. Watson gave us a great inspection yesterday. He examined all the kit and worked us over thoroughly. We are all pleased to be rid of Landry he nearly killed the men, marched us off our feet day after day and he would follow along in his motor car. Am afraid he was very much disliked in the Brigade.

I heard about Milton Sinnett the other day, one of the Gaspé boys saw him, he was feeling well and wearing dark glasses. I believe the gas did him some harm. They also said he was waiting for his discharge and would be sent home. Still they may keep him here on the base doing light duty.

I was so sorry to hear of Lewis Fitz's death. Poor Lewis, he would have been better off with Bert wouldn't he. I am so sorry for the poor kid.

Well I will say goodbye and so long will write from France as soon as I can.

Love to all and tell them not to worry about me. I am going to be alright and pull through.

> *Your loving son*
> *Leo.*

Southampton

September 14th, 1915

Dear Mum:

We have just received instructions about letter writing and we have to be so careful once we get over, we can't give any names of places where we are, any transport names, or mention the name of your regiment, etc., etc.

Yesterday aft. I scribbled a few lines to Stella and enclosed snaps of myself. Well we marched off at 3:30 and took the train from Shorncliffe, we took quite awhile to put the transports aboard so didn't get off until after 7:00. We came right through then passing just outside of London and arriving in Southampton at 1 a.m. (we had a good night's sleep on the way). Then took all the transports and ammunition wagons off and got through at about 3:00, we then rolled on the floor and slept with our heads on our packs and had a good rest. Who would have thought a year ago I could sleep on a freight shed floor without even a blanket.

I can't say when we are leaving or where we are going, we are about to go up onto the wharf and can't see a bit of the city and nobody can see us. I am willing to bet that nobody knows at Southampton that we all passed through last night and are out here today.

The system they have for handling troops is really wonderful. Everything is done just so and to see the way the horses are put aboard and caged-up and the transport wagons swing up and are put in their places without a sound or even an order from anyone. It's great to be down by the sea again and watch the old gulls flying about; you would almost think you're down in old Gaspé.

I am feeling well and happy and you people must not worry now that I am over, I know that it will be hard not to, but what's the sense, it won't do you any good and I am going to be alright.

Love to all,
Leo.

૪૭

Leo's Unit shipped to France on Sept 15th, 1915.

L<small>EO AT HOME IN</small> G<small>ASPÉ BEFORE THE WAR</small>

Back Row (L–R): Leo's brother Bert; sisters Marion and Zadie

Middle Row (L–R): Leo's Mother Zoe, his father Charles Sutton, and his sister Gertie

Front (L–R): Leo's sister Lauretta and Leo

STELLA   ZADIE   GERTIE

THE LeBoutillier home today. Now called L'Ancette, it is a bed and breakfast that retains most of the original house unchanged

THE GIRLS HOCKEY TEAM – ZADIE IS 3RD FROM RIGHT
(SEE LETTER TO MUMS DATED MARCH 23RD, 1916)

THE BANK OF TORONTO BUILDING IN GASPÉ HARBOUR, WHERE LEO
WAS EMPLOYED PRIOR TO HIS ENLISTMENT IN THE CANADIAN ARMY

FOUR-MASTED SCHOONER AT THE LEBOUTILLIER WHARF
DRIED COD DISTRIBUTION FROM GASPÉ CONTINUED INTO THE EARLY 20TH CENTURY

LEO AFTER HE JOINS THE CANADIAN ARMY (1914)

Mobilization parade in Montreal (1914)

S.S. Cameronia

The ship that took Leo to England (See Letter to Mama dated May 13th, 1915)

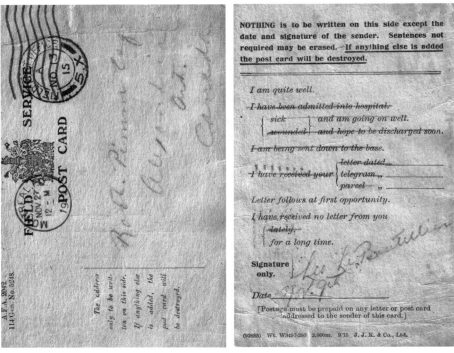

POSTCARD AND LETTER FROM LEO TO HIS SISTER ZADIE (1915)

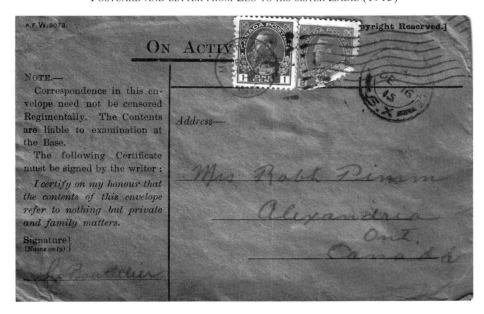

PART II

❦

France 1915 - 1916

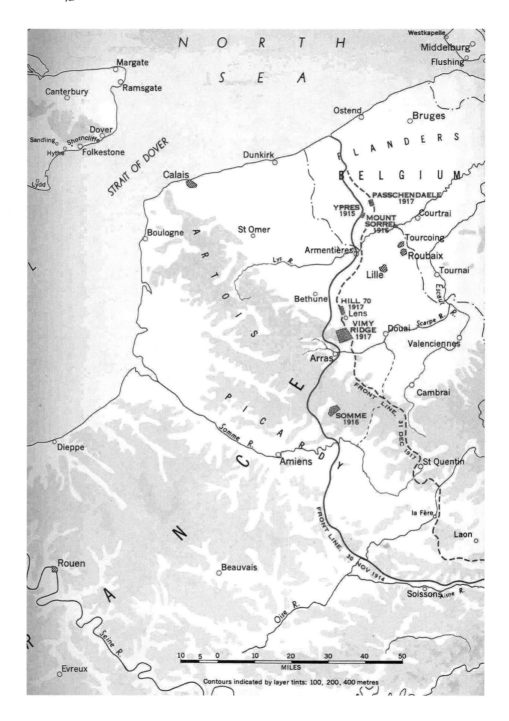

CHAPTER 5

In the Trenches

The 24th Battalion, Victoria Rifles, arrived in France at Boulogne on the S.S. Queen on September 15th, 1915 as a part of the 5th Canadian Infantry Brigade, Second Division. They were on the front line by September 28th.

After landing at Boulogne, the 24th moved to St. Omer by train, then marched 13 miles to Hazebrouck, from there to Bailleul where the guns could be heard, and finally to Locre, their jumping off point to the trenches of the Kemmel sector.

At the time, a Montreal newspaper reported that, as the 24th moved into the front line for the first time, they passed a Military funeral in the churchyard opposite. The "dead march" was the music that introduced them to their new home for the following eight months.

With the arrival of a second, unseasoned Division to join the First Division, the Canadians were formed into a Two Division Corps and were assigned a less active area of the now 400-mile long Western Front, stretching from the English Channel to the Swiss border.

The 24th Bn. arrived in September 1915 and spent the winter of 1915-1916 in the trenches holding the line, exchanging artillery shells with the enemy, and experimenting with trench raids.

The German leadership were first to recognize the need to revert to defensive positioning and built trench systems around "strong points," sometimes giving up ground so as to effect rational defensive arrangements. This early recognition of what was to come was thought to be a result of the necessity to subdue the Russians in the East while holding in the West, as well as recognizing that military technology at this time favoured defense over offence.

On the other hand, Allied decision-makers operated from a different mindset, namely they were in France " to throw the rascals out." In consequence, most of the action from 1915 until 1917, when some success was finally achieved, consisted of the allies battering away at superbly designed defensive positions with almost nothing to show for it except huge casualties on both sides.

The 24th Battalion, a unit of the 5th Brigade, Second Division, like all other Canadian units was part of the British army and, were it not for Hughes's badgering, could have been dispersed throughout that army where needed without regard to nationality. As it was, the Canadian units were maintained intact, although sometimes the units were parts of different British armies.

Leo was assigned to the signaling unit of his battalion. Signalers laid and repaired telephone lines, ran messages, and were trained with signal lamps and flags, as well as manning the telephone. The unit telephone was located in a dugout designed to be as secure as possible so as to protect the headquarters, its officers and HQ communications.

In 1915, Leo writes letters in pencil from the dugout when he is not manning the telephone. Ink and inkwells were unavailable in the trenches. Manning a telephone in a dugout as your principal job certainly contributed to one's longevity at the front, so long as the front remained stagnant.

The 24th rotated in and out of the front line at the Kemmel sector during that winter. Supposedly a quiet front, the Kemmel front had no full scale offensive action during this time, nevertheless sniper action and artillery fire, accentuated by a self-induced "active defense posture," reduced their numbers by 505 casualties before they were relieved in April.

(Date blacked-out by censor, but written by Leo during the last two weeks in September, 1915)

Dear Papa:

I wonder if you got my last little note written since I left Sandling, I won't say where it was here.
Well we got on board the ship at 5 PM and sailed out. We had quarters on the same principal as coming across but remained on deck all-night and slept on a roll of rope rolled up like a dog. The passage was fairly rough and it rained all the time, they say they had an awful night in the hold a lot of the

*fellows were sick and had no place to sleep so were
over the floor every where. I think I had the best bed
of the lot although I got an awful soaking; we got off
the ship about noon, and hung around the harbour
all day unloading the trucks. We then marched about
five miles and slept in tents, started next morning
early and marched to a station about six miles off. We
then loaded all the trucks and kitchens on the cars
and left about noon, we were in boxcars about 35 men
in a car. I slept the day and half the night sitting in
the door with my feet hanging out, we stopped here
and there and had coffee that was prepared by the
French for us as we came through. They called it coffee but there was more rum than coffee. About mid-
way out the guard took 4 of us into his little compart-
ment and we had a sleep till morning on the floor. We
picked up the Battalion on the way.*

*We left the train before dinner and started
out on our march, it was as bad as the retreat from
Mons, we had nothing to eat till dinner time and set
out again in an hour, the men fell out one after the
other, they were walking all over the place, if you
could have seen us we were more sheep than soldiers.
I gave my bicycle to the section and let them ride in
turns to get rested. We kept up our reputation though
and didn't let a signaler drop out, but what a job
we had, some of the fellows got so all in that we took
their equipment away from them piece by piece until
they were walking along in their shirt sleeves not carrying a thing. I had two rifles most of the time but a
lot of us were doing that. The officers were very good
also and helped some of the fellows along. At last we
arrived here about 8 PM only having the one meal in
24 hours. We passed Gen. French's H.Q. and passed
the Prince of Wales. We were now in billets and will
remain here for a few days I am told.*

*How do you like my writing pad? It's all I
could find this morning.*

*I am feeling fine not a sore or an ache any-
where and last night after we arrived I went down*

town and bought some French bread and butter and fruit came in about 10 and had a good sleep.

I think I am fit for anything that's in front of us.

I wish I could tell you the places we have been through and where we are now but it's impossible, as all the letters have to be censored before they are mailed.

I will try to write often to you and when I can't write I will send one of those cards.

Love to all and don't worry am feeling quite well, content and happy. We may be some days before we are in the trenches yet, so are quite safe. We could see them shelling a Zeppelin last night, also can hear the guns but that's all.

Your loving Leo.

I didn't mail this yesterday so will continue with a few more lines today.

Yesterday aft. I went down and had a swim. It did seem good to get into the water again even if it was only a little lake. I hadn't had my clothes off for five days.

I came in around 6 PM and had to go on duty right away. I am bicycle orderly between Bde. H.Q. and the Bn. And we are 24 hours on and 24 hours off pretty hard, but I don't mind it, I wanted to go to church this morning but couldn't get off.

I was just reading in the Mtl. Gazette about Gen. Hughes visiting the trenches, I think if he was out there today he would have found more doing, the way the guns are roaring.

I was out on a message today and met some of the (word blackened out) boys of another Bn. who started the march when we did and are only arriving here now, poor fellows found it pretty hard.

Well bye bye again love to all.

Your loving soldier boy,
Leo

Kemmel Front, Armentieres

September 30th, 1915

Dear Everybody:

I am sitting in my little dugout with the receiver of my phone strapped to my ear and supposed to be very busy but am not overworked after all.

We have been in this district where the whiz bangs occasionally whistle over but never do any damage and the only time you hear a great of deal of rifle and machine gun fire is after dark and then they do rip across "snap whistle and crack" in real earnest but it is awfully tame to what I expected. One would think that by even going into the trenches you would be killed but with care and a little luck I think you could live as long here as you would in Gaspé.

I just told you I was not busy but I had to leave this letter for nearly an hour with a rush of messages, then went off duty for a while and am on again until 6 a.m. and it's only 1:10 so far.

We have a peach of a dugout for a station. Two bunks in it and a little table on one side of the wall, a stone floor. Oh, you could almost think you were in some office.

Joe Cockfield and I have this station together and we run it by 6 hour shifts. During the 12 hours from midnight until noon. Then we break up the 12 hours from noon till midnight into 3 hour shifts.

I bet you are all delighted with the war news these days. Isn't it great! We will have the whole lot of the Devils on the jump before long.

I don't mind the shells or bullets a bit. I thought I would be scared half to death when I got up here but we have been brought up to the front bit by bit and now we are in the thick of it we are used to it. It's good sport listening to the big ones coming. You can hear them coming through the air nearly a half minute before they land so you have lots of time to take cover and even if you lie flat you always escape unless the thing lands on you. The hardest part is at night. There are so many snipers around. The Devils are everywhere. One of our chaps got one last night. This sniper took a pot at him so he waited nearly and hour for a chance and let him have it. Poor Mr. German is hanging over a limb strapped to the tree yet. I suppose he will remain there until the rats eat him.

I can't say a Devil of a lot in these letters. Now, I will have to remember things until I get back again.

I got Mum's letter of the 15th today. You always seem to be worrying over me. No danger I will take care of myself. I won't put my head over the trench to see what's going on. If you want to know how long you will last just put your hat on a stick and count the holes in it in 5 minutes.

I expect we will be going to the rear for a rest soon now. Mama asks about Joe Cockfield. Well, he is a very nice chap. His father is a retired railway Inspector who was working in the southern States and Mexico. Joe was born in Mexico. His father is a Canadian and his mother from Scotland. They came over to England about the same time as we did and have been in London and Folkstone all the time so as to be near Joe. I had dinner one night in Folkstone.

*It may be awfully hard for me now to get let-
ters through so don't worry as I have said often before
I will do my best to write every week or even send one
of those cards. But always remember, "No news is
good news". You will always be advised first thing if
anything happens. I am anxious to hear from Mama
soon, she is in Alexandria now. Tell Bert to write and
give me all the news about the moose and where, if
any, were killed.*

*I am quite happy and like my work awfully, it
is interesting hearing all that is going on all the time
and I am nearly always able to pick up the war news
going along the line. There are just the two of us at
this station so we are just about our own boss so are
quite happy.*

*Love to all and write soon. Did Stell get the
music I sent and the snaps? The only trouble with
our dugout is that the mice run all over you when you
sleep. I am always being awakened with one running
over my face or my neck but I guess we will have to
get used to that also.*

Kemmel Front

Monday, October 11ᵗʰ, 1915

Dear Bert:

*It is a long time since I have written home but
I guess you all understand it's pretty hard to write
letters these days. I sent postals through the other day
that I hope you got.*

*I have a bunch of letters here – M's, 15ᵗʰ Sept.,
S's 19ᵗʰ, G's 22ⁿᵈ and L's 26ᵗʰ but none from you yet
Bert.*

*The last letters, you know, we were in France.
Well I am now on my second tour to the trenches. We
are 6 days in and 6 days in rest billets. But to tell the
truth I would much rather be in the trenches than out
in that rotten little town. You know you are quite safe
here. I have a peach of a little station and as safe as
a church unless she blow us up with a mine or drop a
shell on us. You are also safe out in the open trenches
if you keep your head down, everything is a solid as
can be and the only way they can get our men is if
they shell the trenches and knock the sandbags away
and then open machine guns on us. But whenever
they start that we just call our supporting artillery
and they say, "Duck your head" and you will see the
German trenches fly and they soon calm down their
artillery and we rest in peace perhaps for 2 days. Our
artillery is wonderful, they could knock the devil out
of the damn Huns when they like.*

*Did I tell you in my last letter I had a box
from Mrs. Hodgson? She sent me jam, soup packages,
coffee, candy, cigarettes and little box of matches and
a little towel and a piece of soap. I wrote and told her
I was awfully glad to get the soap and towel because
it reminded me that I had not had a wash for 5 days.*

*There's not a thing to do in rest billets. We
were out with a pick and shovel one day burying telephone lines and a few hours on the phone at HQ and
that is all we did for 6 days. I wonder where all the
amusements/concerts and YMCA's are we heard so
much about?*

*It was Stell's birthday yesterday and L's on
the 4th. Tell them I did not forget them. You can also
tell Stella I went to confession and Communion on
the 9th in a little Belgian Church so am quite a good
boy now.*

*Ma and Marion are now in Alexandria. I hope
they have a good time. How is poor old Martha, we*

never hear anything about her now. Does she still say, "toast crusses" and who is her beau now? Tell her not to forget me as I will soon be home with a German helmet that she can wear to Church for a hat and Fritz Ville is losing some of its citizens. There will be no one left in Gaspé soon with the people leaving and dying. Gertie asked if I needed anything. Well I wondered if you could send a little box from home with cake and a few little things. Also a pair of socks and a few cigarettes. Not that I need these but it would be so good from home.

I haven't kept any of my extra clothes. Too heavy to carry around. I only have a change of socks, my Greatcoat, sweater, rubber sheet and blankets. We get a bath and clean clothes whenever we come out of the trenches. It is funny to see how many things the boys have left along the road. Some had extra boots and God know what but it's all along the road somewhere now.

Well Bert, how are things at home? How is Trixie looking? I suppose you will soon be training her now. I hear you had a very lot of bad weather for your farming. You should see the way people over here do things. Drive a horse with one rein and all the devilish looking turnouts you ever saw. The people don't seem to mind the war a bit. You will pull through a town that has just been shelled, big holes in the streets but still the women are wandering about their work and don't seem to care. I hope you can read this, I won't write so long next time.

Love to all,

Leo

Kemmel Front

November 5ᵗʰ, 1915

Dear Stella:

> *Here we are again I have two letters since I last wrote Gertie and Lauretta. You had never told me Dr. McGuire was going to enlist; it was quite a surprise when I heard he had been refused. And did I ever tell you I met Edgar Lephron in the trenches I was sitting down in my dugout and this fellow was standing in the trench waiting for the Sgt. and I thought I knew him so called out hello Edgar the poor kid nearly dropped he was so surprised,*

> *Lauretta asks how many Germans I have killed well perhaps she will be surprised if I say I am damn sure I haven't killed any and you might tell those who are just over here and haven't had a chance to charge the devils that they haven't killed any either or couldn't say for sure that they did.*

> *No we are not hanging over the parapets shooting day and night like most people think.*

> *In the first place you do not see anything to shoot at as I am damn sure the Germans don't put their heads over unless at night and then we bang away and I don't know if we hit anything or not. And during the day, if we put our head up to look around, its good bye to us too. You see it is all snipers and artillery work, we rain shells over on their infantry and they slam them back at us. And then when we feel like taking their trench we run across and put the bayonet to them and drive them out. So you see the infantry in this war is just fodder for the guns. But we wait till we go forward and then we will have the work.*

(Leo included a sketch showing a German surrendering to our charging hero.)

Our old trenches are in an awful mess, mud to your knees and in some places almost to your hips. I am lucky to have my little dugout so comfortable so if I do get wet we have a fire to get dry again but some poor chaps are in an awful mess.

I am sorry to hear Bert's potatoes were so poor, too bad on a year like this,

And Erskine has enlisted and Leslie Langlois, it will do them good, but I hope they will never have to come over here. And Camille is off also; I wish I had known as much about this game when I had the fever as I do now. I don't say I wouldn't have joined; I am still pleased I did but I would have known what to join and what I was up against.

I received the cigarettes OK and was glad to get them, I am smoking one as I write this gee but it is good. I also have Martins letter you enclosed and I will write him soon, I have written quite a few letters this last week. Catching up at last.

I am feeling quite well and up to the mark, and quite happy. I now draw all my rations raw for my station and cook them myself. We brought in some oatmeal this trip and I have porridge in the morning today we had a forequarter of lamb what do you think of that? I cut it up and made lamb chops had a few potatoes and fried them and made tea, some feed.

Well love and kisses to all your dear ones and don't worry now and write often. You don't know what a letter from home means over here. My God you can't imagine how we look forward to a letter. Get Mama to write whenever she comes home.

Good bye,

Leo

Censor A.J. Wooley

Kemmel Front

November 11ᵗʰ, 1915

Dear Lauretta:

   I was awfully pleased to get Stella's letter of the 20th and one from Mama of the 19th. I think I have sent a postal since acknowledging them tho' we are now in rest billets for a few days, and doing a bit of visual signaling but the rest of the time is spent in hanging around doing nothing. I would much rather we be in the trenches all together. Altho perhaps this makes the time go a bit faster having a break in the trenches which was not very nice at times but we must expect mud if it will rain continually.
   We were issued with very nice rain capes the other day. They are really too good for the trenches. I have a good mind to save mine for when I get home. I believe we are to have goatskin coats, knee boots very soon. They dress us well don't they?
   I heard from Mrs. Amy this week.
   Bye, bye. I am quite well and getting fatter every day, happy etc., etc.

Your old Leo.

Love to little Bob, old Bob, and Zadie when you write.

I wrote to Percy Hyman the other day. Ask him if he gets it.
   I don't expect Papa's new building will be much of a success as things must be awfully dead but after this damn thing is all over and I am home again we will patronize it. Last week in the trenches was very quiet with the exception of a little artillery and aeroplane fighting. We, didn't do much else but eat I think I told you we did all our own cooking last week bringing the oatmeal in with us and having porridge every morning. My, but it was good. The only discomfort we had was the mud now and then.

And all the boys are enlisting. Well it was some surprise when I heard the names of all that were going.

What is the Bank going to do for men? Mr. Leonard will have his hands full getting through alone.

I had a letter from Len and Leo Martin, I think I will enclose a letter to Leo in some of my letters home because I have to put a stamp on it for the States and I can't go to the trouble of getting stamps in this damn country.

Kemmel Front

November 21st, 1915

Dear Zadie:

I am a poor sort of brother not to have written you before and now little Robert Sutton must be nearly two months old, I have often thought of you Zadie tho. And am proud to be uncle Leo. I am sure Bob is quite proud of his baby boy and I hear all the time from the rest of the family what a fine child he is.

Now lets us hope it wont be too long before I will be able to see my little nephew and that then he will sure be a fine strong healthy boy.

I received Marion's letter telling me about her housekeeping, I am sure the little change has done her a lot of good; she was talking about taking a run to Montreal. It is too bad you were not married a year sooner eh Zadie.

I am still living and expect to for a long time yet, unless I run into something bigger than myself. Its not a bad life you know if you could only have fine weather and get out of the mud and water which is up to our knees, you can't imagine the dreadful state the trenches are in, and if we were not equipped as we are with hip rubber boots and short fur coats I am sure it would be impossible to live, but we are quite comfortable.

Last week was the liveliest we have had since we are in the trenches, it was one thing after another but I had the best of luck as the dugout I was in fell in on me and I was almost buried alive. It took an hour and some minutes before they could dig me out, but I escaped without a scratch, things will happen you know and I am just about the most lucky animal alive. The same thing happened to two Sigs of another Bn. and the poor chaps were dead in three minutes. Don't mention this at home they would fuss for a year.

Mrs. Hodgson has been very kind to me and has sent me a box every fortnight. She has asked me to their home if I should get leave at Xmas or at any time I can get leave. I don't suppose I will be able to get to Eng. till January or February. Oh for a good wash and general cleanup and best of all a good meal and a nice bed.

I am feeling well and strong and happy and am taking care of myself—so don't worry. Give my love to little Robert and tell big Robert to write if he gets the time.

Hoping your little family is in the best of health.

Your loving Bro.

Leo

Festubert, Givenchy

November 21st, 1915

Dear Papa:

    I have recd letters from Lauretta Oct 28th Marion 30th and Stella Oct 30th.

    Stella wrote from Matapedia she was having her teeth done up there and going back to New Carlisle, Marion was still in Alexandria but suppose she is now back with you.

    This has been a very lively week for me in the trenches, but we have enjoyed it immensely with the exception of the water and mud that is not so pleasant. I have been moved up along the line a bit when a little more is doing, so have lost the peach of a dugout we had at first, but I suppose we must all have our turn in the comfortable and uncomfortable stations.

    Joe is still with me and we make the best of it together and make trench life as easy as possible, also our stay in the trenches has been shortened and we are only 4 days in now and 4 days out.

    While in the trenches we have hip rubber boots and are now wearing our short fur coats that are awfully warm. I wish I could have a picture taken to send home, but there is no chance of anything like that in this district.

    I had a box of cigarettes from Percy today; I wish you would thank him for me. I wrote to him a few days ago. I will also send Mrs. Amy a card now and then.

    I am glad to see so many of the Gaspé boys coming forward it is time they should show a leg

*isn't it and will certainly do a lot of those chaps who
haven't run anything a world of good. I am so pleased
I enlisted when I did and have been through the mill
of making a soldier, if I had waited I only would have
to go now and they haven't the stuff left, which they
sent over in the previous Battalions.*

*Lauretta says the people are saying about the
piece in the Star about the Gaspé platoon, what are
they vexed about because they called them fishermen
or because they are encouraging the boys to enlist?*

*Stella said she sent me chocolates but I
haven't yet received them I hope the come tho; Stella
says Mr. Calles was in very bad health I hope he is
now better again and I also received the magazine
Lauretta sent.*

*I suppose you people have any amount of snow
by now, I wish we were having Canadian weather
here instead of this.*

*Well this will have to do for tonight as I am
being relieved now and am off for a good sleep.*

*Hoping you are well, and Mum, will be back
again with you soon.*

Your loving son,

Leo

Kemmel Front
December 2ⁿᵈ, 1915

Dear Papa:

*I received your nice long and interesting letter
just as I was leaving for the trenches again after four
days in billets.*

I am now moved to another station along our front, have an extra busy one this time, and have been rushed since we came in, today we have had seventy messages and some fairly long, but it all makes the time go and that's the chief thing just at present "kill time".

I am better off this time as far as a dugout goes although nothing like the little home we had first which I used to tell you about. Our trenches here are also much better and it's now possible to keep dry without rubber boots to your hips, so we are all thankful and quite happy.

I was glad to hear Archie had enlisted poor Archie I wish he had come with me, he certainly will make a good soldier, I haven't seen Sgt. Snape but met one of the boys of the R.C.R.'s who knew him. Len is in the 60th I am afraid by all reports he is with a pretty tough lot, but he will most likely be a N.C.O before long and Joe Clarke is going back to Gaspé I thought all the time he was with his regiment in India, he has done his best anyway I suppose.

Yes, I sent Mr. H Hyman a postal some time ago. I saw him just before we left Montreal, and promised to let him know how I was getting along. I also wrote to Percy some time ago.

Well November is over and peace has not been declared, I always said the war would end November 1915.

I wonder how long it will last, here we are only 60 yards away from the devils, if either side puts their head up in daylight it's pretty sure death, at night we blaze away in the darkness and never know if we hit anything. The artillery seem to do all the fighting and our battery's are wonderful we can put over three shells for every one they hand us and place them within a five foot ring if we tried, when they are doing a little bombarding it's good fun to watch the sand bags fly out of their parapets. I think we can put it over old Fritz any day as far as shooting goes and everything else when we get good and ready.

I am feeling fine and stand the whole works OK. I wish I could tell you more of what we are doing and life in general but the censor is too well (up) on his job.

Love to each and every one of you. Will write again before Xmas.

Your loving son,

Leo

Censor J.A. Ross

Kemmel Front

Dec. 5th, 1915

Dear Mama:

I haven't written to you forever so long, but now I am sure you must be home, so here goes.

I will start off by wishing you and Papa and the rest of the family a very Merry Xmas and a new year that will soon bring many changes from the present and will find us all in our happy home before many months.

Xmas will be a bit different for me this year but we are all going to make the best of it and make things as merry as possible.

It happens we come into the trenches again the day before Xmas, so the day of feasting will be spent in a dugout. I wish I had my first old station back, with it's fireplace and all, but I don't mind as long as the boxes come in good time so there will be lots to eat. And we will celebrate next year.

I received Gertie's letter today full of good news, and also Martha letter which was enclosed, it was very nice of her to write and I enjoyed it so much, I almost died laughing where she reminded me of all the names I had for her, and the songs about Phil Sweetman, anything like that does sound so funny just at present.

Don't forget to wish old Martha a Merry Xmas for me and old Jim and Susan and all the old friends. And you took a room in old 27. I wonder if you saw the room I spent last winter in, how we laugh at our training in Montreal now. We used to think we were just it because we had to walk 8 miles with a rifle. A good dry bed on the floor with three blankets was hardship in those days. Regular hours and meals. I would like to have a talk to some of the fellows who are going through the same thing now and are kicking.

That's some staff at the B of T. I am glad I am not there. Do you ever hear from or about Bisset I wonder if I could get his address, as I would like to write to him.

The weather is a bit warmer this week, awfully wet. This is a fearful country. But I am happy and don't give a d---- if it snows ink as Bob used to say.

I am going to bed now as it is 4.30 a.m. and I have been on this phone for 20 hours with no sleep. In fact I have done 23 hours out of the 25, so we will roll in now for a while.

A merry Xmas to everybody.

Your loving son,

Leo

(Ps. I go to Mass every Sunday and we are out and candles often—a good boy eh?)

Censor J.A. Ross

Kemmel Front

December 6th, 1915

Dear Zadie:

Just a line to wish you and Bob and Robert Sutton a Merry Xmas.

I wish I was in Montreal this year so I could run up for Xmas with you but I am afraid I am just a little too far away this year.

My last letter from home said that Mama and Marion had left you, I am sure you will miss them for a while now. Never mind, we will all be home next summer. We are still at a standstill over here. Don't seem to be doing anything either way, just holding the line. I wonder how long this is going to last?

The weather has been a bit better this week. Rainy but warmer and the trench we are in is a much better one than the last so you can see we are quite happy.

I suppose you people have about a foot of snow by now. I wouldn't mind a good Canadian winter here a bit. In fact, I think it would be much nicer than all this rain and now damp cold. I have just had a crack at a rat with a hammer. The old devil was sitting up on a sandbag by my neck and I swear was as big as a cat. I hit him an awful bang and off it runs. Not hurt. I believe they are German Scouts the way they act and the mice run over your feet and face while you are asleep. They take charge of the dugout and are good housekeepers.

I hope, dear Zadie, you are quite well and also baby. Wish Bob a Merry Xmas for me and every good wish and luck to your little home.

Your loving brother,

Leo

಄

The results of Canadian military action in 1915 and early 1916 were mixed. The Canadians were attempting, like all British forces, to carry out strategic aims using unsuitable tactics and without the necessary equipment. In addition, they had no previous familiarity with the kind of opposition they were facing.

The Canadians were never faulted for their willingness to fight or for their courage while doing so. However they were criticized for their democratic approach to British military customs and were considered by British Officers as having an undisciplined approach to war.

It was a fact that as the Canadian forces joined the already experienced British they found that many positions of authority were, or had to be, filled by British officers. This gave rise to some tension between the more democratically inclined Canadian "other ranks" when bumping up against British cultural differences. In fact "colonial" when describing Canadian forces was often the view taken by some British officers.

Some of the recent immigrants from Britain to Canada, who had returned with the Canadian army, while considering themselves British, had emigrated in the first place to take advantage of upward social and material mobility in Canada, that was not available to them in England.

In so far as some British officers were concerned they were astonished at the demands made on them from people who seemed not to understand the definition of a "Colonial."

Maneuvering the Canadian Divisions as a Corps alleviated this situation. That meant that all Canadian forces with the exception of Cavalry were kept together as one unit and with the appointment of Lieutenant General, The Honourable Julian Byng, to command. Byng who was subsequently in (1921) invited to be Governor General of Canada, was the seventh son of the Earl of Strafford, The fifty-four year old Byng was innovative and approachable. Although British, he met the need of Canadians to have a identity of their own.

In addition, the experience being gained by the Canadians themselves meant that more and more of the officer corps were Canadians. Eventually, after the success of "Byng's Canadians" at the battle of Vimy Ridge, and the resulting promotion of Byng to Army command, a Canadian, Arthur Currie replaced him. For the first time ever there was a Canadian controlled national force, much to the disgust of some British generals who found themselves being questioned on strategic decisions involving Canadians. Currie as head of a national army, even though it was only of corps strength, did exercise this need to know.

In the end Currie had to do as he was directed even if he had misgivings, but he did influence how the Canadians were to carry out their assignments and he did demand and receive the support from the "back office" British army units such as artillery, and the supplies needed to achieve results from the tactical plans he made, while conforming to the High Command's strategic decisions.

At the time that these larger issues were being decided, such as what place Canadians were to take in the prosecution of the war and who was to lead them, Leo was continuing to learn his trade on the job. What he saw was not always to his liking. Disappointment at perceived lack of progress in concluding the conflict was the first negative emotion discovered in his letters home.

ॐ

Kemmel Front

Jan 1ˢᵗ, 1916

Dear Bert:

What does Jan 1ˢᵗ, 1916 look like to you, I know it looks damn strange to me and almost impossible.

I am seeing the old year out and the new year in, but not in the same way as most other people are, I have been on the phone since 10 PM and have to remain here till 4 AM, 2 more hours so I should worry.

At 12 sharp everybody pressed down the key of their buzzer and held it down for five minutes, the worst noise imaginable. The buzzer is exactly like the vibration in old Nedra[1] and you can know how 30 or so buzzers the same as that would sound.

I am going to try and get a pass to visit a little town tomorrow; I believe they have moving pictures there for the troops, so it would be a big celebration to go to the movies on New Years.

I was awfully pleased to get your letter the other day; you must keep up the good work and write often now. Today I also got my box of fruit cake and allies delight I believe tho there is another box on the way yet, its so long since I heard of them being shipped that I have forgotten what was really coming. The cake was fine although there was no icing left it was all in crumbs and stuck to the paper. I suppose they had it in some warm place. I think the cake is grand also the delights, I did enjoy home made cake once more Ethel Renauf sent me some beautiful candy and a pair of socks I had beautiful cake, and candy from Russ this week also. My but we have lived cake and candy for dinner five o'clock tea and supper.

We haven't seen a bit of snow yet; my first green Xmas and I hope the last.

I was glad to hear Bisett was well again, I hope he writes to me, as I would like to hear from him. I would have written to him but don't know his address. How on earth can they get along at the bank, is Paul there yet or has he enlisted, I suppose that everything must be dead.

Well old boy, I can never find anything to tell you in my letters so will say good night and here's wishing you a happy and prosperous new year.

Your loving bro,

Leo

(P.s. Read Stella's letter of Dec 8, has Charlie Davis enlisted?)

1 ⁰ Nedra was the LeBoutillier's family motorboat.

Censor PW Woolsey

Kemmel Front

January 14th, 1916

Dear Gertie:

    I haven't had a letter from home for weeks. I suppose the Canadian mails must be held up somewhere again and some of these days I will be receiving about half dozen. We are in rest billets again and I am on the phone 2:15 a.m. It is always an enjoyable hour when I write home isn't it? Last tour in the trenches was very nice weather and rather quiet with the exception of a trench mortar bombardment which made things a little lively for a time.

    I got my Xmas number of the Standard that was very interesting. We have movies now at our YMCA 3 times a week. There was a great rush the first night. Doors opened at 6 p.m. and we lined up at 4:30 and the show didn't start until 7. It was very good. We are having another tomorrow night so I suppose there will be another rush. Do you ever have Charlie Chaplin in that movie palace of yours? He is very funny and I am very sure would amuse the people there.

    I had a letter from Dick Luce or at least a note. I must try and get down the line and see them. I believe they have just had one week in the trenches and are now going through further infantry training. Don't forget to let me know when you hear of a Gaspé man getting plugged. As I would never hear of it here unless he was of our own Battalion.

    I met a very nice chap in Sandling Vigo (I won't say that it's spelled that) from Jersey who has been on the Gaspé and New Brunswick coast. He was in the 26th. Poor chap got his some time ago. We have started with our leave but only a few will be going at a time for a few weeks. I believe we have our draw

*tomorrow to see when our turn comes. I hope I have
some luck and won't have to wait for 6 months or so.*

*Had a letter from Alma last week. Geoffrey
has been back on leave and has returned to the Front
again. I am feeling A-1 in every way with the exception of my teeth which I am having attended to at
the ambulance hospital. They have very good den-
tists and everything up to date. The only trouble is
I am much too fat. I believe I have gained about 10
pounds.*

Bye, bye. Love to all.

Your loving bro.

Leo

🙳

Leo did, as he reports, have to reconnect telephone lines destroyed
by shellfire and to do so required being exposed to enemy snipers,
but most of the time the dugout was immeasurably more secure than
manning the wall of a trench. That the young man became bored
with this role and volunteered for something different is perhaps
understandable, although when his job changed to Scout in 1916
and it became known to his family, he had a lot of explaining to do.

Below, Leo writes on *Signals Forms* to his sister Stella. He thought
it better not to test the sense of humour of the censor so he leaves
off those sequencing numbers and other official marks that would
identify the letter as an official communication.

🙳

Kemmel Front

Jan 19th, 1916

Dear Stella:

*I haven't any paper so I have to hit up the
army for a few message forms. I was going to fill it
out like a real message but find I can't put my station
call or the office stamp, sender's number or reply to,
number.*

I received two letters today yours and Mamas 31ˢᵗ and 2ⁿᵈ also the box of snaps which are swell I have them by me now and write two words and eat six biscuits its great getting things from home. There hasn't been an awful lot to eat these last few days. We are in reserve and had a bath that I enjoyed as long as it lasted but you can't get much of a scrub in four minutes can you?

I had a bit of an accident the day before yesterday but nothing serious. A rifle fell off the wall in the hut and landed on my head that made a slight cut. I have been going around with my head all bandaged up like a wounded hero. I got me off a darn old carrying party tonight though. Which I am very pleased about.

Ask Mama if she remembers a chap named Dwyer I told her about when I went home last year (the American). Well he is the most popular boy in the regiment today. Has done some very good work that I will tell you about later; he has certainly turned out to be some boy.

I like my new job fine and have had it pretty easy except one night they called me in the trenches a line got smashed up and it was pouring rain and I had the worst time finding the other end there are so many of these lines lying around and this special one had about 20 yds. cut out of it. I am d_ _ _ _ _ if I could find the other end but did put it OK and got soaked from head to foot But as soon as you come in you draw your ration of rum and then go to bed and awake dry and OK.

It's too bad I never got the box you spoke of with the pipe chocolates and Oxo. I think tho it's the only one I have missed.

Poor old Johnny Bannier is sick again well I hope he recovers this time and that xxxxxxxxxx when his letter reaches you.

It's awful about poor Chas Kennedy. There is a wonderful business that will go to ruin now I suppose. What could have gone wrong?

Lt. Chas. Garneau—well Charlie has done well.

Love to all. I am quite well,

Your loving Leo

Kemmel Front, Baillems

Jan 21ˢᵗ 1916

Dear Mum:

I received a large mail today 5 letters and newspapers 3 letters were from home yours Marion's and Lauretta's. Gertie's I received a few days ago, I have also had a letter from Alma, Jeffrey has been to London on leave poor Alma seemed so pleased to have seen him.

We drew in our section and I got 14 out of 32 not too bad but I don't suppose I will see blighty for a few months unless a few of us get killed off and give the others a chance. Old Sgt Robins is in London now lucky boy.

I have received all the pictures of my nephew and I think him a fine child, only I wish he would stay awake while he has his picture taken anyway the little devil always has his face screwed up and eyes shut, but he will sit up and take notice in a month or so I suppose. The other snaps of dear old Gaspé are awfully nice, Stella and Isabell in the canoes, everything so peaceful and quiet and the beautiful water then the one of Cecil's camp your picnic to Cape

Derosiers it all looks so different to this damn country flat as a pancake nothing but knocked down houses cut off trees and mud to your neck.

We had a concert given by some of the boys of the first division, it was very good, a minstrel show and they had some excellent jokes on the trenches and everybody in general, one I remember, they asked the whole class where Flanders was, each described as nice as he could being in Belgium etc. but it did not satisfy the fellow who asked the question, so he told them where Flanders was "one half was under water and the other half in sand bags" and he isn't far out.

I am again with Joe in a new station a fine place in the front line, but a new dugout just built of this curved corrugated iron so it's a strong as a church although a shell took a few sand bags off the corner today and broke every damn wire we had, just back of the trench, I got them fixed up again tho in about 20 minutes, the trouble was in getting the right wires together. No I didn't get a photo from Russ, she told me to send it, but I have no place to carry around photos so it is safer keeping till I get back

And Charlie came to see Paul and never let you know, well he is the limit, what did he come to see Paul about? It must have been something or Charlie wouldn't come to see him ever.

You were asking about socks well when we go to the baths now which is about every ten days we get a clean pair for our dirty ones besides that we carry 3 or 4 pair in our pack to change if they get wet, so we are doing all right, they are adding to our comforts every day and by the time the bunch who are training now get here it won't be like war at all.

Poor old McKenna was killed the day before yesterday, he was at Loyola with me.

When any of you write to Minnie tell I knew the gloves were from her and I have made good use of them. But I did think they were from Isaiah's mother because Stella was there and she just put her card in Mrs. Macguire but we should worry I have the gloves.

Poor old Mike still on the job eh? De banker and de farmer. Bert can tell Mike I often think of him.

I thought J. de St Croix had enlisted you said about two months ago he had left. It must have been funny Lauretta getting the candy. I pinned the little badge Sister Redemptor sent, tell Marion to thank her for me when she writes.

Love to all the dear ones and yourself dear Mama.

Lovingly,

Leo

Kemmel Front

January 27ᵗʰ, 1916

Dear Zadie:

It's really a shame that I never write to your family but I always think you get to hear from me through home and I imagine you much nearer Gaspé than you are. So please forgive me, Zadie dear. It's not that I never think of you and Bob and now the two children and I have all the little snaps you sent and ones from home of little Robert except two which I gave to Mrs. Hodgson as she had none.

I have letters from Gertie of October 15ᵗʰ and December 3ʳᵈ and your last one of January 1ˢᵗ and I was so pleased to hear all about little Marjorie and that little Robert was so well and getting on so beautifully Your home will be a great change from the

*time I left won't it. I often plan on my homecoming
and how wonderful it will be – getting back to you all
and settling down to a natural life again. Let's hope
it will be this year.*

*I'm always going to write to Bob but in the end
give up the idea as I know he would like a letter telling him of our life out here and what we are doing.
But it's all impossible and I'm sure these letters don't
interest him.*

*I had a great old time in London. Was out
with Herbert for two days and spent two nights out
with them. They also took me to the Gaiety Saturday
afternoon. I went out to Westcliffe for Xmas and
Boxing Day and enjoyed it very much. Mrs. Hodgson
is a little dear. I wish you could meet her soon and,
Zadie, the two children are wonderful little kids. My,
they make me ashamed of my childhood days. They
were so willing and Jim was ill and wasn't allowed
downstairs and the child played up there all day and
never a word. If that had happened to me on Xmas
Day a few years ago I would have cleaned up the
whole house or driven everyone mad.*

*Mrs. Pimm's little Billie is also a sweet little
girl but she is much younger than the two others.
Poor Mrs. Hodgson had a Colonel for Xmas besides
me so it made quite a contrast. Colonel and Private at
Xmas dinner. Still we didn't fight.*

*I saw Alma and Geoffrey and Cecil Gaffney
were on leave also. He arrived while Alma and I were
up at Shorncliffe seeing Cecil.*

*I took in a number of shows and had numer-
ous meals at the Regent Palace, Criterion and a few
other places. Tell Bob Piccadilly and the Strand are
still in the same old place.*

*It was pretty hard coming back but I soon got
into the old way gain and now just as crawling as
ever I was. Haven't had a bath or change of clothes*

since London, December 27ᵗʰ. We are now out of the trenches and going through a training. I understand it will last a few weeks. I am not sorry a bit being out of the line as the weather is very cold and little snow on the ground. We are very comfortable here in a nice billet and the French people are so kind. Can't do enough for us. We have the kitchen for ourselves and a room upstairs to sleep in. Every morning we come down they have a cup of coffee waiting for us. I would like to stay down here until the end of the War and this is what half of the men at the Front have all of the time and think they are at war. The poor infantry though don't see much of it.

Mrs. Hodgson has been very kind to me ever since I came to France. She has sent a parcel every week and Xmas she sent a big box with a lot of good things but it arrived about a week before Xmas and I had it all eaten away before hand. Poor Mrs. Hodgson thought me an awful villain and was almost going to send me another.

Well Zadie dear, excuse this paper it has been too near a cake I'm afraid. With much love to all and I wish you luck and to the children.

Your brother,

Lills.

Kemmel Front

Return to St. Eloi Craters

March 23ʳᵈ, 1916

Dear Mums:

I have received your letters of February 27ᵗʰ, Lauretta's and today yours of March 5ᵗʰ, Stella's of March 2ⁿᵈ and also the box of biscuits with the 5 boxes of Players cigarettes. Gee, the cookies were great!

*I have eaten the whole pail full. Damn near alone.
The cigarettes were also a Godsend as my mouth was
burned up from smoking those issue ones.*

*Your letters were all very interesting and I am
looking forward to the results of the Hockey match
and the success of the Carnival. I do hope Lauretta
puts it all over those girls. Tell her not to forget the
end of the stick in the ribs.*

*I was thinking the other day what fun it
would be to arrange a match with the Germans in
"no man's land". Wouldn't it be some match—Canada
versus Germany? Perhaps we will have a little bayonet match one of these days that will do as well.*

*The boys were home on leave gain. The lucky
Devils. I suppose they might as well enjoy it while
they can, as when they get out of here they won't be
running back every few weeks. We have been here
over six months now and through the worst part of
the year. I haven't even gone back for a rest but I am
well and strong and in the best of spirits and expect
to see " the whole game through" as they say. We have
had some very nice weather but it has turned cold
again. I spent most of my spare time in the last two
days under the blanket to keep warm. We are now in
reserve billets.*

*Had a great picnic the other night – rat hunt-
ing. Got a dog and about 10 fellows with sticks and
shovels and we would dig them out of their holes
and then the dog would grab them. By dark we had
slaughtered four. A big evening's hunt wasn't it. It
has moose hunting beaten a mile.*

*I wrote to Mrs. Amy today I hope she sends me
a cake now. Leave has started again but there are so
few to go at a time that a fellow hasn't much chance
of ever getting away. Still England will be all the
nicer in a few months I suppose.*

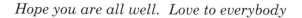

Hope you are all well. Love to everybody

Your son,

Leo

Zillebeke, Mount Sorrel

April 27ᵗʰ, 1916

Dear Mums:

I have sent you a Postal since receiving Lauretta's letter of April 2ⁿᵈ. I have also received your letter Mama dear of the 5ᵗʰ April so I will answer your questions first before I forget. You asked how my head was? It healed up in no time. It wasn't much of a cut you know. Just a mate for the other little cut I got for building my camp when a piece of the top of a tree lit on my dome. Of course you know now I am in the Scouts and having a fine time. You also said you had not heard from me for quite a long time. I suppose one of my letters must have gone astray but I am writing oftener now and when I haven't time to write a letter I will send cards.

I am afraid the Canadian papers will be saying a lot about the fighting around the xxxxxxxxxxxxxx. They always exaggerate things so and make you think things are much worse than it really is. Old Leo will take care of himself. We hear great rumors of the war ending May 27ᵗʰ or during the summer Let's hope it is true. I wouldn't mind a bit arriving in old Gaspé in a few months.

We had a little excitement last night. Fritz tried a little attack but was severely beaten. Bombs just sailed over at him and then artillery opened up and it was just a steady roar for an hour and a half.

I wouldn't give much for the bunch of them that ever got back.

We have been having beautiful weather lately – a little too warm to be healthy as there are so many smells and the ground is just covered with insects which crawl all over you if you haven't ordered that vermin repellent I asked for I wouldn't bother as I got some from Alma and can get fellows going on leave to bring me another when this runs out. Of course, if you have ordered it send it along, it will always be handy.

Tell Bert to write and send me the plans of his new stable. I am anxious to see what he is going to build. I am going to go through the Royal Stables if I ever get back to London on leave. I understand they have visiting days for the public. I hope Lauretta's knee is O.K. again and she is about. Also Marion is over her grippe.

This letter is getting so dirty I think it's best to quit. Hoping you are all in the best of health.

Don't worry.

Your loving son,

Leo

(Ps. Saw Edwin Garrow (Lieut.) in the R.E. the other day but did not speak to him.)

៸៰

Having moved from the Kemmel sector, the 24th was sent to re-serve at Wyschaete, then almost immediately to Renninghelst, just south of the Ypres salient near the St. Eloi craters. These craters had been created by British mining operations with the idea that if you could not subdue a defensive position by charging it, you could burrow under it and blow it up from below. This resulted in those occupying the position being blown up with the ground they stood

on, ground that now became a huge crater. Ironically, the resulting crater often provided a better defensive position than before its
deadly rearrangement.

In contrast, the Ypres salient was not considered a quiet sector.
Exposed to higher ground on three sides, the lower ground was wet
and uncomfortable and had been abandoned in 1914 by the Germans
in favour of the surrounding higher ground. The British occupation
of the salient was primarily a political decision. No one wanted to
give up any Belgian city—even if the enemy did not want it. As the
war progressed, Ypres was totally destroyed by shellfire. British and
Canadian forces initiated two major battles and numerous smaller
actions, and managed only to maintain their position in the salient.

After holding the craters and Voormezeele until the end of May,
the 24th moved to Zillebeke, Mount Sorrel, and on June 8th took over
the line at Maple Copse and Hill 62 (named for its height above sea
level).

ॐ

Ypres Sector

June 12th, 1916

Dear Lauretta:

> *We arrived out of the trenches this morning at
> 4:45 and still safe and sound. We have been through
> a four days of hell and I am very thankful to be one
> of them still. I understand we may have a couple of
> days in the line again and are then going back for
> our long looked forward to and needed rest. So you
> people need not worry for some time. I dare say you
> have been wandering through pages of casualties and
> worrying yourselves but never fear; Leo is going to
> come through without a scratch. I received your let-
> ter of May 22nd and was very pleased to hear from you
> and that you had received the ring off a Whizbang.
> I gave you full particulars in my next letter. I have
> had a lot of souvenirs more caps of shells and hunks
> of shrapnel but I have thrown everything away, too
> heavy to carry. We had a ten-mile walk this morning,*

after that trip in the trenches and, of course, it had to be raining, but they had rum and hot coffee ready for us and then we rolled up and slept till 3 p.m.

That was quite a ride you had around the bridge, but hard luck to have you have the tire go bang. Today I received your box. It was in the best of condition and good. I haven't eaten very much yet, because I have just received a box from Mrs. Hodgson, chocolates, cake, apples, I have been eating all afternoon.

I had a letter from Mr. Leonard a few days ago and will answer it soon. If you hear of any casualties of the Gaspé boys, let me know, as I never know except the chaps in our own Bn.

June 13th

Had to leave this last night and go to bed, as I was pretty tired. I've been reading an English paper and they are giving the Canadians great praise. I bet The Montreal Star has published some delicious stories. Just got some great news, the rest of the trenches that we had lost, have been taken back by the 1st *Div. I guess they took advantage of the bad weather as it's been raining the last two days. We also captured a lot of prisoners. The last night we were in, a Hun came over and gave himself up. One of our listening posts saw him coming and waited for him and then when he got near enough he jumped up and got hold of him and ran him up the trench at about where we were dug in (it was no trench). The poor Hun everybody wanted to get a bayonet in him, but they got him safely to HQ where he would be of more use alive than dead, for information. He tells us he has been in the regular German army for ten years and has been through all the fighting, but has never met with anything like these last twelve days. We gave them five days steady bombardment,*

*for which the 24ᵗʰ held the line. He was very funny
trying to speak English, "that shells! Me no stand."
If you have been following things up you will notice
that the poor Canadians have been into everything
since they came to this front, the same old story, isn't
it? We have had nearly as many casualties, as the
British Army in France, and we are only a handful of
men compared to the British or the Imperials (as we
are all British). But, never mind—it's old Canada
forever.*

*Write soon again, as I now must get washed
and shaved not having done so for six days and no
bath for four weeks. Gee, I have to stop and scratch.
Good-bye old sister, I am well, and will write again
soon, and we will be out of the line for a rest in a few
days. Also to get up to strength again, some our platoons came out with two men strong.*

*Love to everybody, and don't worry, this will
be mailed in London,*

Leo

Zillebeke

June 21ˢᵗ, 1916

Dear Papa:

*We are out of the trenches again and still safe
and sound. When I last wrote it was the day we went
in, that is six days ago. We took over the won ground
and held it. Things were in awful shape and artillery
fire fierce, day and night. Although I must say it was
not as bad as our previous tour. Still, I have pulled
through and we are now having a well-deserved rest
that I hope will last a few days anyway. When we
left our last trench, we had been in six days, and then*

*we had two days rest and rushed up to here where
we dug ourselves in almost, and remained four days.
We were taken out for a long rest we were told but
only got two days and rushed back again for six days.
Well, we came out again last night and let's hope for
a week now, anyway.*

*I only wish I could have kept all the souve-
nirs I picked up, but it's impossible to carry them.
I brought out a German greatcoat, rifle and gave
them away. I have kept a few buttons and lapels of
the coat, which I will enclose and the coat of arms is
F.R. that is Friedrich Rex, I think. I also have some
German letters and a bit of a diary, which I will give
to you. I am using one of their water bottles and a
canteen and I have a N.C.O.'s bayonet and a haversack, ammunition, respirators and God knows what
all.*

*We had a lot of wounded prisoners also, and I
can say our boys treated them like ourselves, carried
them out and gave them anything we could; it's very
funny to see fellows who like myself have often said,
oh, I would never take one of the dogs alive. All that
but when a fellow has been through it, he changes
his mind and is ready to share his last lick of food,
cigarettes with the man who is down, even if he is our
enemy. A lot of them were young chaps and seem to be
gentlemen, like ourselves. One case, a little chap only
sixteen who had been wounded and been lying out
there for four days, and when we found him he was
quite pleased with his treatment and said Canadian
gentlemen.*

*I can't seem to get in touch with any of the
Gaspé boys and we fear the Mounted Rifles were completely cut up. I wonder where LeGrand is. I think
Luce was with the staff, so he probably will be o.k. I
am anxious for news from you.*

*I have so many letters here to answer that I
have no idea which I have answered and which I*

*haven't. One from Gertie visiting in Alexandria, I
hope she is now back with Zadie and baby. Mama
says in her letter of the 18th that Mich had left for
Eng. Poor old Mich. I wonder how he will make out
and Stella says in hers of the 30th that you are not
getting Martha back. I hope your new maid will be
satisfactory. I suppose all the work you were having
done is finished and must look quite nice. And how is
Bert's barn getting on?*

*It's too bad about Mr. Scales. Who will re-
place him? I am sure the funeral must have been
quite swell. Stella enclosed a clipping from The Star
of a message had been picked up from four fellows
of the 22nd and wanted to know if I knew them and
where they were. Champney was transferred to the
Engineers and Peters got a commission in an English
regt. Donnelly is wounded in England and Bertram,
a Jerseyman, is away wounded for the second time.*

*I also have a few tickets here I got out of the
ruins of Ypres Railway Station. I will try to get them
home some time.*

*Well, dear Papa, I will close but will write
again in a few days. I am feeling fine. And I think
my nerves are as good as ever they were. That is a
common complaint now after so much shellfire.*

*Love and kisses to everybody. I will write soon
again.*

Your loving son,

Leo

Ypres Sector
June 23rd, 1916

Dear everybody:

I did not enclose the souvenirs in my last letter as I thought they might go astray and it would be better to have items censored, as I will enclose them here.

I haven't been doing an awful lot since I last wrote. That night I went down to the movies and last night we took a walk down town and saw a baseball match in the aft.

Today we had gas practice going through it with respirators on they seem to be very satisfactory.

We have had wonderful weather since we are out and enjoying a little rest.

I haven't heard from you for a long time, I hope Mama and you have not been worrying too much. I know it must be hard nowadays. But I guess it is all over now. I saw Tommy Rowly the other day. He is still Jake.

With much love to everybody,

Your loving,

Leo

Ypres Sector
July 14th, 1916

Dear Mama:

I received Stella's letter two days ago. The parcel of biscuits, chocolates, cigarettes, it was very good and how I did enjoy it. I received a parcel from

Mrs. Hodgson, the same time, so I had such a good feed and didn't draw my supper. We are expecting to be relieved tonight, we have been sixteen days in this tour rather long isn't it? But I don't mind so long as we get that long out. Still, I expect we will be called in again in a few days. It's generally the way.

Yesterday I got permission to go back to Capes Battery, and saw Edgar Bourque and Stanley Hughes, who went to Loyola with me. They are all a fine bunch of boys and have been out about 3 weeks. I was very pleased to see Edgar and he seems to be well liked and getting on well. He helps in their little canteen and is their first aid man, and also does his turn on the guns. We had a great old talk of Gaspé, and the other chaps being new, were of course anxious to know a thousand things about the front, well, I told them all the lies I could think of.

Edgar seems to have known Dooley. Richards' son's sister wanted to know all about him. He also introduced me to a great friend of Dooley's; the poor chap was killed just a few yards from me. Edgar gave me a present of a pair of pants and a shirt. They found me pretty raggy, I guess. But we have been in so long and one night I got caught up in some barb wire and it was no place to lose any time, so I just went through it and left half my clothes behind.

Edgar and I are going to try and get passes next week to go to a little town for the day. I hear you can get your picture taken there. So, we will try.

Well, I have just been detailed for the advance party to go out and take over billets. So we are really going to be relieved. I have been doing some very interesting work lately observing from a point behind the lines with a powerful telescope. It's fun watching Fritz. The other morning I watched three of them working. They were building something. Just then

one of our shells went over. It could not have burst
anywhere near them as I did not see the explosion.
But you should have seen them duck. Yesterday I
watched two officers. They were a great way behind
the front line, but I could see them as if they were 25
yards from me. They were walking about and giving
instructions and doing as much talking with their
hands as with their mouths, the dirty old dogs. I
wish they would show themselves within rifle shot.

The Scouts work is very interesting. I am getting along very well, much more in my line than sitting in a dugout with a phone on my ear.

I had a letter from Jessie Carter today. I
guess she is in Gaspé now and the Lindsey girls are
home. You will all be having a great time this summer.

I was sorry you lost your little girl. It's funny,
old Martha does not come back. I don't believe her old
stepmother can be so very sick.

Tell Bert as soon as he gets time he must write
to me and tell me all about the new stable. He can
draw a little plan of it. And it will be very interesting.

I must leave this and pack up. I will finish it
tomorrow, when things are a little more quiet. Good
night.

*July 17*th

Well, this is awful. I have left this letter go
three days. We were not relieved on the 14th after all.
Had to stay in another 24 hours, but came out the following night and was glad to be back in civilization
again.

We are in a tent this trip. Yesterday was
rather rainy but we got a bath and got paid and had
a meal and a good sleep.

*Joe is now back in England sick, lucky devil.
There are not many of the old boys left.*

*Today is a beautiful warm day. I hope it con-
tinues. I am now anxiously looking forward to mail
from you.*

*The papers are full of excellent news of fur-
ther... We are putting over Fritz in every way.*

*I am feeling quite well and fit and will write
soon again,*

Your loving son,

Leo

Ypres Sector

July 21ˢᵗ, 1916

Dear Zadie:

*After a long wait, I received some Canadian
mail, a letter from Mama and Marion. The mail has
been delayed somehow or other.*

*Well, Zadie, dear, Mama's letter enclosed a
picture of baby, you and Bob and was very good of
the family but you; the baby is a sweet, little thing.
He looks so much better than in those other snaps you
sent, where his eyes were never open. Some boy, sitting up by all by himself. I only wish I could see him.
When will he be walking and talking?*

*Mama's letter said you had received my cards
of the 5ᵗʰ and 10ᵗʰ, but no letter and Marion's of the
3ʳᵈ, didn't mention anything of letters. I wrote one on
the 11ᵗʰ. I wonder if you received it or not.*

*Marion's letter says you have been up river and
making the best of the weather when it is fine as you
have been having horrible weather. We had it very*

*rainy also in June and quite a lot in July, but the
last three days have been fine and warm for a change.
You would never believe it to be summer, if it wasn't
for the crops, which are beautiful and everything is
so pretty. Of course, up the line, it's a bit different.
But, still, about a mile back of the line, there have
been some beautiful houses. I was wandering around
the ruins of a beautiful chateau last week. Of course
now it is in ruins. Just the pieces of walls left, but
the grounds have been wonderful and all of these
old places are surrounded by a moat. I wish I had
the history of the country where it would tell me who
these people were and who lived in these places. It
would be interesting.*

*We were in the line 18 days last tour, but were
expecting the same out, so didn't mind much, but I
hear we only get 8 days out so we will soon be moving
back again, I hope it will be shorter than last tour,
though.*

*I am sure you must have all been interested
in the six-mile race. Bert should have trained up for
that. It would have been great sport. Hard luck for
Manny, though. Tell him to write to me when you see
him again.*

*I see Tommy Rowly quite often and Edgar
Lephron the day before yesterday. I went to see Coffin
in the 26ᵗʰ. He is in the Transport and is o.k. He
tells me Gerald Millar has a good job looking after
an officer's horse of the Trench Mortar. So he is quite
safe. Coffin also saw Eric Edin since he came back.
He was not wounded badly.*

*We have received numerous drafts, but I don't
see any of the G.G. amongst them.*

*We have been doing a lot of training this time
out, making maps (that is enlarging them) and a
lot of work on Scouting. We had a very interesting
lecture on Scouting today given by the Intelligence*

Officer of the Div. In the evening I either go to the movies or play baseball.

I couldn't get to town to have my picture taken as they shelled it for 5 days and we were not allowed a pass.

We seem to be doing very well around the Somme. I hope it continues. I wish I was running things, I would never leave them alone and the reports we get of the fighting down there is that the German casualties are terrible. No doubt, we have lost heavy also. But the Germans say themselves that their regiments were absolutely wiped out.

I am writing to Joe today. He is in Blighty. Lucky devil, and only a form of trench fever. I am sure his father and mother will be delighted as they have been in England ever since we came over from Canada.

Bye bye, Zadie, dear. I am looking for a letter from you. Kiss the baby for me. I am going to write to Bob.

Your loving brother,

Leo.

(P.S. Tell me if my letters have anything crossed out and when green envelopes are opened. L.)

Ypres Sector

July 24ᵗʰ, 1916

Dear Mama:

Received your letter of the 7ᵗʰ two days ago and also the parcel of Kisses. They were very good. We came into the trenches last night again. I hope our stay won't be so long this time. I don't know what on earth to tell you as I haven't any news but just as long as you know I am well I suppose will have to do.

I had letters from Joe, he is in England, and says he is not at all sick. Sgt. Robins has now gone. We haven't heard what it is or where he is. Kind of hard luck in his case as he was waiting for his commission to come through but everything for the best, he is much better away from it altogether, and if he gets to Blighty and gets a good rest, being a little sick, won't hurt him.

You were asking about socks. Yes, whenever you are sending a parcel slip a pair in and those belts are also very good, but don't last any time so they are quite welcome also.

Today has been quite nice. I have had a good sleep this aft. Didn't get much last night and I was out from 4 a.m. till noon.

With much love to everybody. Tell little Robert to be good.

Your loving son,

Leo

ଔ

The Canadian Expeditionary Force was moved to the Somme on August 24th, 1916. The Battle of the Somme is the best-known action initiated by Field Marshal Haig, Commander in Chief of the British Forces. It is also probably the main source of criticism leveled at him by historians. Few commentators have been able to understand why the battle was undertaken in the first place—and why, having encountered enormous casualties, particularly on the first day (60,000 of which 20,000 were killed), the battle was continued for four-and-a-half months.

From July 1st until the 19th of November 1916, when the Somme offensive was finally called-off, the combined casualties totaled more than a million men, equally divided between Allied and German forces. Furthermore, the relative positions of the contending forces remained much as they were despite the massive loss of life during the futile battle.

One justification for the battle made by Allied commanders (offered after the battle concluded) was that German losses came from their "best" units and the Germans had no way to replace these units. The Allies, on the other hand, had their Dominions, colonies and hopefully the Americans to provide reinforcements. Thus, the Allied justification for the failure of the Battle of the Somme implies it was deliberately planned as a "battle of attrition" making the enormous human cost even more sorrowful to contemplate.

ఴ

The Somme

August 3ʳᵈ, 1916

Dear Everybody:

> *I am getting to be an awful correspondent. It's ages again since I have written. I must not say I haven't written, because I have, but failed to mail them. I wrote one letter in the trenches and kept it so long I had to destroy it. Then I find another written on the first and still not mailed, so will have to start over again.*

> *I received all your letters. The last one being from Gertie, I am pleased to hear you received the little souvenirs. But you never said if the trench paper "Vic's Patrol" was ever received and another letter written on the 13ᵗʰ of June.*

> *We have been having very hot weather and I do wish I was home after reading of your picnics and bathing. Oh, for some nice fresh salmon! I wish you would enclose a dollar bill now and then. I can get*

five francs for it, and get something to eat now and then. I am sick of Army grub and our little 15 francs twice a month doesn't buy much. I would also like a nice maple sugar cake like the Lindsay's always make and I used to put out of sight in ten minutes.

I was passing Bde. H.Q. last week and saw Edgar Lephron. He called me in and fried me a nice piece of bacon and made tea. Believe me I had some meal.

Sgt. Robins will be back today. He did not get to Blighty after all. I haven't heard from Joe lately.

The news is still good on all fronts, I don't believe they will be able to stop the Russians and still hold the West. Let's pray it won't last another winter.

Tell Jessie Carter I met a chap from Sidney's Bn. who knew him and he is o.k. I received a letter from her today also, and will try to answer it soon. Does Stella go visit them very much this summer?

I am still making out well in the Scouts. We have done some very interesting work lately, which I wish I could tell you all about. I am quite well and healthy and strong. So, no room for worry.

Your loving,

Leo

The Somme

August 10th, 1916

Dear Papa:

I have been going to write for days but I am always letting another day go by without doing it.

I find it so hard to find anything to write about. It's always the same old story, in and out of the trenches, every tour we come out minus a few, and about every second tour a bunch of new drafts, and that's the way it goes.

We had an inspection today by our new Commander. It reminded me of the olden days at Sandling. I think we make a pretty good showing, but of course, haven't our arms drill down like the old days of training, being nearly a year since we have done much of it.

I am quite a sport these days. Got a whole new outfit this time, from my head to my feet and I think I needed it as I was in rags. Clothes don't go very far out here.

August 12th

Well, I had to go off without finishing this again yesterday. I was away on pass all day to a town not far away. I had a pretty good time and went to the movies in the afternoon and had a great dinner, roast pork, chips, peas, gee it was good, after this army grub, it's the first day since I have had off since Christmas. Got back at 6 p.m. when we were marched off to a concert, which was pretty good, given by the Royal Flying Corps, got home at 10 p.m., and this morning we were out for a march with full equipment. I guess we did about 12 miles. We were walking from 6:30 to 10. We have been doing a lot of marching lately. I guess getting in trim for a long one, as I wonder are we going back from the firing zone for a rest of a few days. If we do, I will be borrowing more money from Mrs. Amy. I had my picture taken yesterday and will send you one. It will be something to laugh at as I know they will be rotten, just postcards.

Sidney Carter came up to see me the other night. I met a chap of his Bn. and I told him to tell Sidney he met a chap from Gaspé who called himself Leo. So, the other night he came around to see me. He is looking very well and seems to be a nice chap. We had a long talk of old times. Their Bn. has been hit very hard also. It doesn't take long to get rid of a thousand men, does it?

I am writing with a German hat on. I must try to send it to you. It will make a nice little souvenir, if it can get through.

I received a letter from Percy Hyman and was glad to hear from him. I received the candy Lauretta sent. I don't know if I have acknowledged it before or not. We are having beautiful weather and I have been sleeping outside for over a month every night. The nights are cool, but we can sleep comfortably on a rubber sheet under us and a greatcoat over.

I hope you are not worrying. Love to everybody, and I will try to write more often, your loving son,

Leo.

The Somme

August 18ᵗʰ, 1916

Dear Lauretta:

I received Zadie's and Mama's letters of July 26ᵗʰ and 31ˢᵗ, they both arrived at the same time while we were out of the trenches. I was very pleased to hear from Zadie and get all the news of baby. He must be a cute kid. The drawing of his hand was very funny. Also the little note to Uncle Leo. It is too bad Bob can't get down for a few days anyway. But it's nice to know he is getting on so well.

It's a shame to be missing all these nice motor trips to Peninsula and Haldeman isn't it? But, never mind—next summer will surely see me home! We have had some very warm weather, but I cut my trousers off just above the knee. It is very much cooler, but makes it kind of hard crawling on patrol. I have to wrap my bare knees up with sandbags. It's great for marching, though, and fooling around.

I had my picture taken and am enclosing one. The chap with me is Bill Dwyer (no, we were not drunk). But, don't we look funny? Bill's eyes are jumping out of his head and I seem to be all falling to pieces. Still, you will all have a good laugh. I am going to try to get some more taken some of these days with my shorts on.

I am also sending you a copy of the Vic's Patrol. Did you get the last one I sent in June?

We expect to have only a short tour in the trenches this time, so will write soon again.

With love to all,

Your loving brother,

Leo

(Ps. I am feeling quite well and fit)

The Somme

August 23rd, 1916

Dear Stella:

I have just received your nice letter written in Barachois, it's sometimes seems so long between letters from home but I just think it's the mails.

We came out of the trenches two days ago, and I had heard that all the Gaspé boys were over here very near us. I had an awful tramp to find them and at last located them and saw them all but Archie who was in the trenches. He is in the Scouts. It was great being amongst a bunch of Gaspé boys again. It seems so long since I have seen anyone from home. They all treated me like a king and I would have rather gone right back into the trenches with them, then have to separate again. Last night I got away again and went up to their camp but was only with them a couple of hours as they all went into the trenches, all but Len, who was working in the Orderly Room. I saw them all march off, a fine looking platoon they were. All were very cheerful and anxious to get into it and see what things were like. I hope they have it quiet until they get used to life and then I will have no fears of 15 Platoon showing the Bn where they were born and brought up.

I can't give you all the names of the chaps as I know you all know them as well as I do, and they are all looking in the pink of condition and so nice and clean with new uniforms and all dolled up.

Erskine was in great form and looks splendid; Ralph is a fine soldier and I know will soon make a name for himself. Frank Cass also looks well and was eager to get into the line. The two Boulay's, Dunn and Sinnett, Coffins and Bert Moran, and Guignon and the rest of them, looked up to the march and were quite happy.

Len said he was going to try and come down to see me tonight and bring Archie with him. I hope he does, oh, I saw Archie's corporal today, and he has many a good word for him. So, on the whole, I am quite proud of our Gaspé soldiers.

Oh, who do think I saw today? Dick Luce. The first time since I am in France, he has a good job and is looking fine. He says Le Grand has been with his regiment in the trenches all the time and is quite well. It was just the greatest luck; I ran across him as he was riding by with an officer and I was wash-ing near the camp, we soon recognized each other.

I don't expect to see any of the Gaspé boys again as we will be a long way away from each other.

I have mailed you a snap taken not long ago and a copy of the Vic's Patrol. Also let me know if you get a little parcel.

Well, as usual, there's nothing to tell you about. I am quite well. That's all.

Your letter was very interesting and I guess you have had a nice time in Barachois. Of course, there is not much amusement. I was glad to hear about Corinne and their little family.

Bye-bye for now. Love to everybody. I guess Len will be writing to you soon. I haven't received that last parcel you sent yet. It's funny that the Gaspé parcels never get here.

Your loving brother,

Leo

The Somme

September 2ⁿᵈ, 1916

Dear Mama:

Received Marion's letter today with the cute little snaps of baby. My he is a little darling; the pic-tures of the veranda with all the dear old chairs were nice to look at also. Reminds me of better days.

I last wrote home on the 30ᵗʰ. We haven't been doing much lately, except marching and training. Today I started a course in Lewis machine gun. It's

*good to know a little of everything. It's very interest-
ing. Some time ago I took one in Bombing and bayonet fighting. So, with Signalers and Scouts and the
rest of them added on, I might make a soldier some
day. Not forgetting a year's experience in the trenches
at dodging shells that is most valuable.*

*Well, Mum, I guess I have seen enough of it. I
wish the H_ _ _ _ it was over!*

*I had a letter from Len yesterday and he said
one of the boys had been wounded. Patterson, I believe. I hope they are not having it too rough. I met
Caldwell of New Carlisle yesterday. He is in the 26th.*

*We have been having a bit finer weather these
last few days, and it is great to be back from the shellfire flares, etc. If it wasn't for the soldiers everywhere,
one would think there wasn't a war on.*

*Isn't it great that Rumania has joined with
us? I think it's going to make a great difference.
Austria will find herself in a bad way soon, and if
Russia marches through Rumania on Bulgaria?*

*I wish they would send us to Salonika for the
winter or East Africa. I don't suppose you met a Miss
Waters, who was down with the Garrows this summer? She is a friend of Dorothy's and her brother
was a Pte. in the 11th Platoon but was wounded some
time ago. Was glad to hear Bert was getting on well
with his farm. Tell him to write when he gets time.*

*Bye bye. With loads of love from your loving
son,*

Leo

The Somme, Courcelette

September 9th, 1916

Dear Mama:

My last letter home was September 4th. That afternoon I received Stella's letter, but haven't heard from you since. I guess I will get a letter the first Canadian mail we get again. Things are rather mixed up as we have been on the move now for 16 days.

I am glad to hear Bert is all through with his farming at least hay, tell him he must take a trip in the woods for a change as well as a rest, he can shoot my moose also this year. Gee, I wish I could join him on good hunt. What glorious life, never mind I have to try and get a few Germans during the hunting season instead. We are allowed to shoot them all year round, but it's not such good sport as moose and caribou as they shoot back.

I think poor Gaspé will be dead for certain this winter, if everyone is clearing out. Poor Stells, what on earth are you going to do with yourselves and I know you are going to miss old Mick. Anyone heard what he is doing in England?

I told you in my last letter about meeting Dick Luce. He is a lucky devil; always back with Div. H. Q. riding around on horseback. I believe he is now attached to the 4th Div. as his officer was transferred when they came over. I wonder if you ever got the little parcel I sent you. It would most likely come through Art's officer, I suppose. The next souvenir I must get is a German officer's spike helmet. I don't know how we will carry it around, but will have to find some way.

I am feeling in very good condition. We have done a lot of marching, but the marches were short.

The longest day was about 15 miles. Some times we only do five. We are now in a little wood where there are huts for everybody. But I prefer sleeping out in the open when it looks like rain we make a little tent out of two rubber sheets. The weather has been very nice and everybody is in the best of spirits, including old yours truly.

Hoping for a letter soon with good news of you all, I hope Zadie is not thinking of leaving for some time yet. With much love to everybody, don't worry.

Your loving son,

Leo

(Ps. Received your letter of the 20th today.)

∞

The Canadian Corps was not involved in the Somme offensive until early September. The Second and Third Divisions moved toward the heavily defended town of Courcellete passing through the line defended by the First. The Fourth Division was still with the British at Ypres.

Offensive operations were being conducted on the "Two-up and One-in-Reserve" configuration. This meant that for each Company, two of its three Platoons led the attack, with the Third supporting the charge and carrying supplies close behind. This configuration was duplicated in each correspondingly larger formation – Battalions, Brigades, Divisions, and the Army Corps being similarly arranged.

In the battle for Courcellete, the 24th was in support of the 22nd and 26th Battalions. Under "Two-up and One-in-Reserve" configuration, the supporting units carry bombs (the Mills bombs) forward and the wounded men back, then change places with those making the initial assault. They then move up to throw bombs at the enemy and risk becoming casualties themselves.

Leo earned his Distinguished Conduct Medal during the Battle of The Somme and the subsequent Battle of Ancre Heights (which became the generic name for the back-and-forth fight for the trenches named by the Canadians as "Regina" and "Kenora").

∞

The Somme

September 20ᵗʰ, 1916

Dear Papa:

It is now a way past time for lights out, but my candle is still burning and I must not see another close without letting you know I am still safe and well in the land of the living. It has been a hard costly few days and you dear ones must be worried to death. But I am one of the very few lucky ones and I am back in rest billets for a few days. I sent you a postal on the 14ᵗʰ, but have not written since the 9ᵗʰ. Such a long time ago, we had one day's march after that till we arrived at xxxxxxx, the 11ᵗʰ, 13ᵗʰ and 14ᵗʰ were spent in looking over our new ground. It was a pretty hot spot, but everything was so interesting, being on new won ground, all the old German dugout trenches and the towns that have been captured on the night of the 14ᵗʰ we went into the line as our own big guns pounded away preparing for the morning at 6:20 they put up a fearful barrage and at 7 our boys were at 'em. My Bn. was not in the charge, but they were first support to the advancing Bn.'s and kept them supplied with ammunition and bombs. The second day was the same. They laboured on and lost heavily. On the 17ᵗʰ the old Bn went over after them and although it was only a small scale, the British report it as being as brilliant an adventure as has been seen.

The Div has made a wonderful name for itself, in which our Bde can claim a large share of the honour, and our old Bn.'s name won't be forgotten. Some of the Bn was relieved on the night of 17ᵗʰ and the rest came out on the night of 18ᵗʰ and some sight we were as the last two days it has been raining and the ground is so cut up that mud is by no means scarce, we arrived at the Div Camp at 4 a.m. We were met by our officers who couldn't do enough for the men. Fires were burning to dry our clothes and rum and hot tea

*was handed around. The next morning we took buses
to a little town further back where we are now resting
for a few days. I hope I haven't said too much in this
letter but if it doesn't go it will only be crossed out. I
know I could say a lot more.*

*I sent two German spike helmets to England
to be packed and sent home. I hope they arrive o.k.
Also a belt. I was pleased you received that little
parcel. I picked all sorts of souvenirs this time but
couldn't look after them. They were all lost again.*

*I received your nice letter today and thanks
so much for the money. I did write to Mrs. Amy for
some money a month or so ago but did not get it. I
think my letter couldn't have reached her. I wanted
some for our march but it doesn't matter now. I won't
need it.*

*Lauretta's letter was very interesting. All
about her trip. I bet they had some time. I also have
Mama's letter of August 20th, so will answer her questions. Sgt. Robins came back to the Bn. He was not
wounded, he left us again for a commission the day
before we went into the line. I haven't heard from
Joe for some time, but hear he is getting on well in
England. I never got the belt Jessie Carter sent. You
asked if they are useful. Well, they are for a week or
two and then the strength goes out of them. We are
pestered with them just at present, such a life isn't it?*

*I got the socks from Mrs. MacCartney and will
drop her line. They were very nice. The parcel was
great and the cake and everything swell.*

*Well, Papa, that suggestion of leave you made
would be all very nice, but I am afraid it would be
impossible. It would take a lot of money and I don't
think such a thing would be allowed to Pte's.*

*They are starting leave again this week, and
now I hope to get a few days shortly. There are so few*

*of the old men left that I couldn't help but get it soon,
but you know in our Bn and even Div there have been
very, very few that have had leave. They have been
letting only a few go in a Bn in a week and then leave
is open a couple of weeks and closed for months. So
it's kind of slow. I will have to say goodnight as I
need sleep badly and it is getting late. With much
love to everyone,*

Your loving son,

Leo

Lens/Arras

October 13th, 1916

Dear Stella:

*It will be some time before this will be able to
be mailed as we have been on the move for some days
and they won't accept any mail anyway. I will scribble away a little now and then and when the time
comes I will have a letter written. Lauretta's and your
letters of the 12th and 16th of September were received
O.K. I was glad to get all the news and that you had
such a good trip to Perce. It must have been a great
time. Stella, you never told me anything about Mrs.
Jopling except that she is a friend of Lauretta's and is
visiting the Lindsay house. Lauretta promised me a
picture of her and tell her not to forget.*

*I had a great laugh over Trixie's misbehav-
iour. Poor Stell, you must have been raging eh? Old
Martha is with you now I suppose. I am sure you are
all pleased to have her again. Give her my love and
tell her to write.*

*Well Stell, I am pleased to get out of that hole
with my life. There is hardly an old man left and all
our Officers and NCOs nearly, gee, it's kind of tough.*

Tell Percy Charlie was killed. Lyons is in England taking out a commission so is O.K.

I am looking forward to leave. All the men drew last week and I was just about the end of the list. Such luck! Still, I am not in a hurry just at present as now the bad weather is coming and I must face another winter. Leave will look good after that time.

I am expecting some good news from you soon so it is not such a bad world after all.

Today we are marching along we swiped a little dog and just put a string around his neck and brought him along. He is a fine little fellow and will make a good mascot.

How is old Tubby and the old Red fellow getting on, I often think of old Ponto.

Say, Stell, have you heard from Russ lately? Her last letter said she had not heard from you in ages. What has become of Esther? I never hear of her from anybody. Have any of the boys enlisted? I received the two dollars Papa enclosed in your letter.

Good afternoon, I will continue this tomorrow.

October 16ᵗʰ, 1916

This poor old letter is not gone yet you will all be thinking me dead

We are settling down to trench life. We came straight up to the line after a six days march but it is a home as quiet a place as we have ever struck. I am sitting down in a trench writing this and there isn't a sound around. I am enclosing a little snap taken a few days after we came out of the line. Some looking creature eh? The weather is beautiful today although a little cold. Reminds one of those beautiful Fall days at home. A shame to be at war isn't it?

By bye

Leo

Leo in France

"TODAY WE ARE MARCHING ALONG WE SWIPED A LITTLE DOG AND JUST PUT A STRING AROUND HIS NECK AND BROUGHT HIM ALONG. HE IS A FINE LITTLE FELLOW AND WILL MAKE A GOOD MASCOT." (SEE LEO'S LETTER DATED OCT 13TH 1916 TO HIS SISTER STELLA)

MEMBERS OF THE ROYAL 22ND BN. OCCUPYING TRENCHES THEY EXCHANGED WITH LEO'S 24TH BN. (SEE LETTER DATED NOVEMBER 16TH, 1916). "I WAS SURPRISED TO GET A LETTER FROM LT. PAUL GARNEAU THE OTHER NIGHT. HE IS WITH THE 22ND; IT WILL BE PRETTY HARD FOR ME TO SEE HIM AS WE ARE OUT OF THE TRENCHES HE IS IN."

'Communication Trench'

So-called because it provided shelter to troops moving up to a front line trench

RELEASE OF A HOMING PIGEON. WHEN THE TELEPHONE DID NOT RING, AND THE RUNNERS DID NOT RUN, YOU COULD SEND YOUR MESSAGE BY 'AIR MAIL.'

"I AM BETTER OFF THIS TIME AS FAR AS A DUG OUT GOES. IT IS NOW POSSIBLE TO KEEP DRY WITHOUT RUBBER BOOTS."

THE 29TH (VANCOUVER) BN. 6TH BRIGADE 2ND DIV. AT VIMY.

THE 6TH BRIGADE ALONG WITH THE BRITISH 13TH CONSTITUTED THE SECOND WAVE FOLLOWING

THE 4TH AND 5TH BRIGADES. LEO WOULD HAVE CROSSED OVER THE GROUND PICTURED HERE SHORTLY BEFORE THIS PHOTO WAS TAKEN

FROM L TO R: LEO'S DISTINGUISHED CONDUCT MEDAL AWARDED IN 1916;
THE 1914-1915 STAR; THE BRITISH WAR MEDAL; AND THE VICTORY MEDAL

NAME.		RANK.	NUMBER.	UNIT.	HONOUR OR AWARD.
LE BOUTILLIER. L.B.		Pte.	65553	24 Battn.	D.C.M.
AUTHORITY.	DATE.	MEDAL LDG-R FOLIOS	33		MENTIONED IN DESPATCHES.
		RECEIPT No.	764	DETAILS. TO BE CONTINUED ON BACK OF CARD IF NECESSARY.	AUTHORITY. DATE.
R.O.2909.Turner.	21-10-16.				
L.G.29824.	14-11-16				
OTHER AWARDS.					
NATURE.	AUTHORITY.	DATE.			

For conspicuous gallantry in action. He carried
out a reconnaissance under very heavy fire,
obtaining most valuable information. Later, he
rescued a wounded man, and carried out several
more daring reconnaissances, also carrying bombs
and ammunition to the front line, He displayed
great courage and determination throughout.
L.G. 29824.

THE OFFICIAL DESCRIPTION OF LEO'S ACTIONS THAT LED TO HIS BEING AWARDED THE D.C.M.

CHAPTER 6

Sir Arthur Currie

Arthur Currie, a former real estate executive from Victoria B.C., had in peacetime made the Militia his avocation. Currie arrived at Valcartier as a Brigadier General where he was appointed commander of one of the four brigades that made up the First Division of the Canadian Expeditionary Force.

Currie is important to this story because he was later promoted to Major General and was the commander of the First Canadian Division at Vimy. It was his influence that made the Canadian contribution as notable as any military unit on either side of that war. Currie was permitted and encouraged by Julian Byng, Commander of the Canadian Corps, who in turn had the confidence of Henry Horne, First British Army Commander.

Canada's bid for military recognition, as led by men such as Currie, was of course made possible by all ranks. For example, Leo volunteered to be a "Scout" (a designation that does not appear anywhere as a formal military rank). The job title of Scout did not really describe what they were—it described what they did. The Scout gathered information.

Men like Leo who engaged in Scouting activities provided vital information about the enemy, what units were deployed against them and what defensive positions needed to be overcome. This information, added to aerial surveillance ground flash spotting, was employed in counter battery work led by A.G.L. McNaughton, a young artillery officer whose groundbreaking skills were considered the most important of all elements leading to victory at Vimy Ridge. Historians consider Vimy as *the* defining event in Canada's national history.

The Canadian approach to fighting the war involved accepting reality on the ground sooner than most other national units that made up the Allied forces. Conditions were difficult and confusing for everyone, but the Canadians seemed to make more practical use of what was available to them than others. For example, some Allied forces were slow to recognize how devastating the machine gun would be against attacking ground forces and that the weapon had changed infantry tactics forever.

Hiram Maxim, an Anglo-American inventor, had tried to interest the British army in a machine gun in 1885, nevertheless senior British generals could not see the new weapon's relevance to infantry warfare while others regarded the weapon as barbarous and "unsporting." On the other hand, the British army in the Sudan did use machine guns, referred to as "Maxims," during the late 1880's.

Hiram Maxim moved on to Germany where he found ready acceptance of his new weapon. The Germans added five more letters to the name calling it a "machinengewehr" and mounted it on a sled that contributed to its mobility. The German Army had already deployed more than 12,000 machine guns when the War began, compared to just a few hundred "Vickers" machine guns deployed by the British.

As it happens, the "Vickers" was really a "Maxim" because after working with the Germans, Hiram had joined with Vickers to produce their version of the machine gun. The British Vickers was equal in performance to the German version but achieved mobility only when disassembled from two parts. What originally seemed like an irrelevant difference in speed of mobility to deploy the heavy gun became significant in WWI. When the war became an artillery duel, pulling a machine gun sled in and out of a dugout to protect it from destruction by shellfire was much easier and more effective than disassembly under a hail of shells.

However, Canadian commanders such as Raymond Brutinel successfully used machine guns in offensive operations by mounting the heavy guns on trucks to achieve mobility and accordingly duplicated the barrage techniques of established artillery.

By 1915, the lighter more mobile Lewis machine gun became available—also an American invention by Isaac Lewis—and Canadian units employed more Lewis guns than British formations to successfully offset German standard tactics.

Canadian Corps Commander Lieutenant General Julian Byng, Currie, and other senior officers with open minds, had observed the enemy always counter-attacked in force after losing ground, thereby exploiting the chaos that existed among both attackers and defenders during the height of the battle. These counter-attacks usually restored the front to its previous position. As a military tactic this was hardly a novel idea. For example, giving ground grudgingly before returning to attack an overextended enemy had been the primary tactic employed by Genghis Khan during the 13th century.

In addition, German defensive strategy was focused on the concept of a defense "in depth" with individual "strong points" sited to support each other. It was necessary therefore to recover any strong point that was lost—otherwise the integrity of the in-depth defensive web would be undermined. Max Aitken, in his book *Canada in Flanders,* laments Allied strategy, saying, "German lines were pierced but not broken. We only succeeded in splitting it up into a series of absolutely impregnable fortresses. These miniature fortresses proved the triumph of the machine gun."

To deal with the expected German counter-attacks, Currie chose incremental, limited objectives and when achieved, immediately set them up as defensive positions equipped with machine guns—*before* continuing to exploit whatever further gains were available. This tactic guaranteed keeping what had been gained and was a substantial morale builder for other ranks.

All operations on the Western Front were extremely violent and bloody encounters and to lose, almost immediately, what you had just gained at great human cost was an all too familiar scenario. Breaking this pattern of "win-lose" would have an immensely positive effect on the morale of those doing the fighting.

The practical application of science was a strong point among Canadians during the War. A.G.L. McNaughton, a junior artillery officer, was familiar with the development of the oscilloscope at McGill University where he trained as an engineer. This device measures the direction and distance from where a sound originates. Employed in groups, the oscilloscope could trace the entire trajectory of a shell, identifying the location of the gun firing the shell to within a few feet.

Put in charge of counter battery work, McNaughton coupled use of the oscilloscope with gun flash observations, and by means of triangulation, pinpointed the location of German gun batteries. Supplemented and confirmed by aerial observation, McNaughton's counter battery work permitted the destruction of the guns before they could be brought into action against advancing ground forces.

At Vimy, half of the Allied guns remained out of the initial barrage until seven days before the actual assault began, and were then devoted to the counter-battery effort. The accuracy of the Canadian guns, and the element of surprise, caused an almost complete disorganization of the German defensive artillery. This was so because the Germans depended so much on their artillery to disperse attacking forces and to prevent reinforcements should an attack succeed. Indeed, during the battle for Vimy Ridge, only two German artillery batteries were unaffected by McNaughton's practical application of science, and thus German artillery batteries were rendered almost completely ineffectual in Vimy's defense.

The "creeping barrage," where infantry advanced closely behind it's own guns thereby protecting it's advance by forcing the defenders to remain under cover until the attackers were upon them, had been tried by British forces two years before Vimy. It had not been used extensively since then because the level of accuracy required to avoid killing your own advancing troops had not been achieved.

McNaughton was able to calibrate the trajectories of his guns by taking into account gun barrel wear, wind direction and strength, as well as any other atmospheric influences. This attention to detail improved the accuracy of the Canadian and British artillery supporting the attack, so that the creeping barrage at Vimy was an outstanding success.

By keeping the defenders hiding under ground until the last minute, and by destroying German artillery before it could be used, some parts of Vimy Ridge, which had withstood every attempt at capture since 1914, were occupied by First Division troops within half-an-hour of commencing the assault. As McNaughton's common sense tactics were being successfully implemented, Canadian soldiers gained confidence in themselves and their leaders to solve previously hopeless and intractable problems of trench warfare.

CHAPTER 7

Scouts in Trench Warfare

Scouts were volunteers and they worked together in groups because they needed to know each other and trust in each other's skills. The volunteers in each "Scouting Group" were drawn from the battalions to which they belonged. Scouts, along with snipers, were the least formal of any group engaged in the war's trench operations.

Scouts operated in groups, whereas snipers were single loners who camouflaged themselves somewhere in no man's land, within or behind the trench system, waiting for targets of opportunity to come to them. Some snipers were so adept at camouflage that friend or foe could literally be within three feet or less of the hidden sniper without discovering his presence. Snipers were equipped with accurate rifles and telescopic sights so the enemy was usually fatally wounded long before he strayed that close. Both sides employed snipers and they caused extreme discomfort to everyone in the front line while also inflicting considerable casualties.

On the other hand, Scouts were groups of no more than seven men that moved about "no man's land" and into the enemy's trench system under the cover of darkness, seeking information and prisoners to be brought back for interrogation.

The Germans did not employ Scouts to the same extent as the Canadians although they did occasionally send small groups to reconnoiter. When opposing Scouts met in no mans land, the meetings were generally non-confrontational. Whoever saw the other Scouting party first generally stayed out of sight—unless the opportunity to take prisoners of the other Scouts presented itself. The Scout's job was not to harass the enemy. It was to gather information and to protect working parties. Harassing the enemy was accomplished instead with artillery, indirect machine gun fire—and if direct intervention was required—by snipers, a "trench raid," or by reconnaissance in force.

The Scout usually worked in a group of two, three, or four but still operated entirely independently as an individual. It was important to support each other when feasible, but Scouts often became separated in the faceless shell-holed terrain of no man's land, crisscrossed by miles of barbed wire in which the Scouts worked. If a Scout did become separated, hopefully he found his way back to his own lines before daylight. Being found in view of the enemy in daylight, often only a few yards away, was not recommended.

The skills a Scout required were steady nerves, stealth and physical strength. Scouts penetrated barbed wire installations sometimes hundreds of yards wide; slipped in and out of German trenches, hopefully unobserved, and returned from whence they came sometimes dragging a wounded companion to safety. It was for Scouting actions like these that Leo earned his Distinguished Conduct Medal—a medal second only to the Victoria Cross. Over 5,000 men served in the Victoria Rifles during the war and Leo's decoration was one of only 20 Distinguished Conduct Medals awarded in the battalion.

Because of the Scout's familiarity with the features of "no man's land" that could be used as guideposts, Scouts were used to lead large formations to and from the enemy's trench system to carry out nighttime raids. Trench raids became increasingly popular as the operational stalemate continued through 1916. The Canadian Corps helped to perfect the trench raid and the tactic's dramatic element of surprise made it a growing source of valuable information.

Later as surprise became harder to achieve, trench raids appealed mainly to senior officers, well back from the front, who felt these exercises were necessary to keep the men from getting stale. Larger and larger reconnoiters in force were mounted often without surprise and for little gain.

In retrospect, some historians have conjectured that the Canadians' nighttime activities were of doubtful value because large force trench raids often resulted in high casualties. But any failures attributed to large-scale trench raids should not be confused with the highly effective work of single Scouts. They used cunning and stealth to crawl through wire to the edge of German trenches, only to quietly withdraw, with highly useful information.

Certainly, Canadian Corps Commander Lt. General Arthur Currie was not confused about the value of Scouts, and he placed high value on the knowledge Scouts retrieved about German defenses and estimated troop levels. Currie was even known to cancel planned trench raids when he discovered he already had the sought-after information from a Scout's action.

Scouts would have completed much of their high-risk information gathering in "no man's land" well in advance of the full-scale assault on Vimy Ridge. Every possible matter that might affect the Vimy attack was exhaustively researched. For example, prior to the Vimy attack, Currie sent Scouts forward to check on a barbed wire belt about which he had conflicting reports regarding its continued existence. The suspected wire barrier was in fact in place, so further artillery action was undertaken to destroy it. Indeed, Currie had written in his summary report that the First Division's failures at St. Eloi had resulted from the failure to remove German wire barriers prior to the attack. Currie did not need to relearn that lesson.

The war diaries written by front line units were most often short on detail with abbreviated accounts of the day's activities. Individuals were seldom identified by name unless they held officer status. Yet the many reports scattered throughout the 24th war diaries about individually named Scouts indicates a much greater level of drama than the few lines devoted to reported incidents.

In the Scout reports where an officer led the group, the reports are more comprehensive, and the activities described were hair-raising. The following accounts are examples of the type of activities carried out by Scouts:

March 15th, 1916

From O.C. 24th Bn (Victoria Rifles) Canadian

To 5th Canadian Inf. Bde.

Sir,

> *I have the honour to submit the following account of meritorious action performed by the under-mentioned N.C.O and men.*

> *On the morning of the 29th inst during the operation of laying torpedoes in the enemy wire in front of the old trench 2.5 right. Owing to a chain of circumstances, 2 Scouts were reported missing.*

At 3.50 am i.e. in daylight, on the conclusion of the enemy's bombardment, no. 66032 Sgt W.C. Westwater with no. 65437 Pte. F.P. Heckbert, a stretcher bearer, proceeded out to J.3 right with the idea of seeing whether they could find any signs of the missing men. A man was seen lying in our wire in front of J.2 Sgt Westwater and Pte Heckbert proceeded down to the place and found it was one of the missing men Pte Juteau who was dead. They then entered J.1 over the parapet. A little later No. 65077 Pte S.J. Bethune and No.35192 Pte E.G. Collins Proceeded out to J.3 right in advance of Sgt Westwater and Heckbert Ptes Mott and Dolphin. The last four named stayed in J.3 right while Pte Bethune and Pte Collins crawled along the ridge crossing no mans land from J.3 Right and from thence to an old French trench. While doing this these two men were observed by the enemy and sniped at. They finally got within thirteen yards of the enemy's wire and found a position there which had apparently been occupied by an enemy listening patrol, as they found empty cartridge cases and used flares. Near this, in the old French trench, was Private Dwyer, the other man who had been reported missing who was lying at the bottom of the old trench intending to wait until dark before going back to our own lines. He did not think it was possible to get back in daylight. Privates Bethune and Collins then returned by the way they came bringing Private Dwyer with them. They rejoined Sgt. Westwater's party in J.3 Right and the whole party successfully returned into J... by means of the remains of the old Communication Trench leading out to J.3. Right From there they regained our trenches. It was then nearly 8 a.m. (signed)

"March 27ᵗʰ, 1916

Fifth Canadian Infantry Brigade

Report on Operations on the xx March p.m. to 6:30 a.m.

Three Scout Patrols consisting of 3 men each made a full reconnaissance of the enemy's wire and the best positions for placing of torpedoes in enemy's wire and the time of approach to these positions by 2.a.m.

The patrol, which reconnoitered in front of H. 4was fired on by the enemy. The parties for laying the torpedoes were organized as follows:

A Patrol of 3 man proceeded by the previously reconnoitered routes across to the enemy's wire in front of H.1 and the old trench J.3 Right and H.4 In the rear of these parties of 3 men that carried the torpedoes. A covering Patrol consisting of 3 men each remained in our own wire at the places where the torpedoes were taken out. The torpedo in J.1 was placed well into the enemy's wire and was ready by 3:45 a.m. It was successfully discharged at 4:15 a.m. on the given signal. Two attempts were made to place the torpedo in front of J.3 Right but were unsuccessful owing to the enemy's activity. A third attempt was made which kept the party out too late with the result that they were still in "No man's Land" when operations commenced. The torpedo was successfully withdrawn and all the men returned with the exception of two. Privates Dwyer and Juteau, the latter being wounded. It was then impossible to go out and look for these men during the enemy's bombardment but at 6:30 this morning Private Dwyer was brought in unhurt by a Scout Patrol, and Private Juteau was discovered dead in our own wire. A report on work of this resolute patrol will be submitted later.

The party's proceeding in front of H.4 were seen by the enemy and bombed, very narrowly escaping with their lives and successfully returned with the torpedo.

This torpedo was later exploded by the enemy's shell-fire while lying in our own trenches. By 4:30 a.m. the enemy retaliated on our trenches, shelling them heavily in addition to sending over trench mortars and rifle grenades. This continued for about an hour and a half – a barrage of fire being put up behind SP.13 old and along the G.T. trenches remaining from H.6 to J.4. The result of this bombardment did not cause serious damage to our trenches and only 6 casualties resulted. The enemy appeared to be very nervous as they continued to send up flares in daylight.

There has been no shelling or fire of any description since then. During the operations the Officer commanding was in E.5 but by 4:05 a.m. all telephone communications had been cut by enemy's fire.

(Signed)

R.O. Alexander,

Major 24ᵗʰ BN. (Victoria Rifles) Canadians

ૠ

The War Diary of the 24ᵗʰ Victoria Rifles for the date May 15ᵗʰ, 1916 contains a reference to a Scout patrol carried out by Scouts Dickson, LeBoutillier and Weinberg in which they encountered a German patrol the resulting action requiring the support of patrol #2. Two days later on May 17ᵗʰ, 1916 the Diary notes that Scouts Miller and LeBoutillier covered a working party performing duties in "no man's land."

CHAPTER 8

Action During 1916 - 1917

Canadian operations during 1916 included the Somme, St Eloi Craters, the Ypres salient and numbers of minor operations. Most of these locations had been fought over continually since 1914 with little or no change to the contestant's positions.

Canadian experiences in the renewed battles in these areas were no different than their predecessors, in that they found themselves in virtually the same location when relieved, as they were when they arrived. However, there was a difference—Canadian senior officers were learning from the experience.

What they learned, included an appreciation of the value of "on the ground" information for planners resulting in a greater understanding of German defensive strategy. Adapting to experience led to the development of counter measures that were implemented in 1917 to some success. The Battle of Vimy Ridge was the prime example of the effective application of lessons learned.

After the Somme the 24th moved to trenches near Bruay, to the west of Vimy Ridge, and subsequently to the Vimy sector where the entire four divisions of the Canadian Army Corps were assembled together for the first time. Here they held a ten-mile front during the last month of 1916 and the spring of 1917. This front, garrisoned by the Canadians was compressed to four miles by the time of the assault on Vimy Ridge.

The months before the Vimy action were a time of careful rehearsal of every phase of the plan. Day after day, walking between tapes laid out on the ground, following as closely as possible behind officers on horseback who were representing "the creeping barrage" that was planned to hold the enemy underground in their shelters until the assaulting force was upon them. For some of the men it was boredom "ad nauseam" and for others a cause for hilarity (they could laugh if marching through horse manure was the worst in store for them). For Byng and Currie this was a time to practice again and again. Currie knew that only extensive preparation could make the Vimy assault a success. Some of the timing between Vimy objectives was down to minutes.

Before the action, many experienced observers from other formations considered the Canadian staff planning to be more than a little "over the top." Following the action, the troops stopped laughing, and the experts joined those applauding the scale of the preparation.

☙

Lens, Arras

November 4ᵗʰ, 1916

Dear Mama:

> *This is Lauretta's birthday, and I hope she is enjoying herself. I am afraid my postal written a few days ago never reached you. I know how you all must be worrying, but Mama, dear, I am still alive and well, and we must all thank God for his protection in pulling me through these last two tours in the trenches.*

> *We arrived in this little town last night after a drive in buses of about 25 miles. It didn't take many buses to bring the remnants of our glorious old Bn. They have done wonders, not only our Bn but also the Bde and Div. In fact, the Canadians, Stell, the little credit one gets does not cover the terrible price paid.*

> *I do not mean by this that we have paid too dearly for what we have gained, because in fact have gained far more than was ever expected of us. My work has been very interesting and our senior officers are very pleased with the little squad. I am sorry to say though, Mama, one of our best men who was out on a job with me was killed. I don't know if I have ever mentioned him before "Crawford." He is a west-*

ern chap from Sask. and knows Percy Patterson and a lot of the Coffins. The greatest lad you ever met. I hope to be able to tell you more about him later.

Last night I received Cecil's letter addressed by Lauretta. He did not say what rank he held in the battery. Is it true he is Sgt. Major? He has certainly improved in his letter writing and I will try to drop him a line some of these days. I received your letter last night also Mama's but it was written on September 7ᵗʰ, such a long time on the way. I know how you all must miss the darling baby, but never mind, we are all going to be home next summer, and such a time we all will have. Baby will be running around by then, won't he?

I am glad the picture was received o.k. No, Mama, it is not good of me or Bill either, but I sent it along so that you could have a good laugh. Bill was transferred to Bde Signalers before coming down here, and I have lost my three next best friends. So, it's kind of lonely coming out of the trenches. If passes open up again, I should soon get mine, although we are attached to H.Q. company and there are so many of them who don't get a chance to be put out of action that there are a number to go yet. We only have three, including myself, in our bunch, but the Police, the Transport and the Pioneers and Sigs are nearly all old men and will take quite a long time to get them all off. Well, it's no use grumbling. It's better to be lucky in other ways than drawing first or second for leave.

Received a parcel from Mrs. Hodgson, and she sends me a paper with a lot about the Canadians, but says nothing in her letter.

The sun has just come out and I hope this is the last of the rain for some time.

With much love and kisses to all and hoping you are all well, happy. Tell Bert to write.

Your loving son,

Leo

(Ps. I picked up a few souvenirs, but hadn't much time to bother with them. Will try to send you a few pictures.)

Lens, Arras

November 7th, 1916

Dear Mama:

I am expecting some mail from home tonight, so will add to this note if it arrives. Did I tell you in my last letter I received a letter from Gertie of October 16th with a few little snaps of baby, which were pretty good? We have been out of the line a few days now but haven't had much of a rest. Always some foolish parade of some kind to keep you from having a little time of your own. I had another day's lecture in bomb training (hope I will be able to throw one soon).

I haven't seen any of the Gaspé boys yet. I would like you to give me all the news you get from them.

Had a letter from Edgar Beaupre a few days a go. He is long way from us and not in touch with any of them.

November 11th, 1916

Have been in the trenches for a few days now but have no mail from you. Yet, a Canadian mail came in the other night and I had a letter from Russ but none from home. I wonder where it can be?

The trenches are pretty wet just now, but it's far better than what we had to go through last year. We have long hip rubber boots and have been issued with the sheepskin and leather coats. I have a leather coat this year. It's much cleaner than the others.

I don't think there is much chance of me getting any special leave; so don't expect to get away till after Christmas.

With much love to all,

Your loving son,

Leo

Lens, Arras

November 16ᵗʰ, 1916

Dear Stella:

Received Mama's letter of October 22ⁿᵈ and yours of October 25ᵗʰ. Glad to get all the good news to hear the helmets had been received. I have the strap and cockade for yours here. I will try to get them over or is it Lauretta's that they are missing on? It was great news to hear they had arrived as the fellows were always saying they would never get them, and I had almost given up hopes myself.

It was also interesting to hear of Rooney, but I would like to hear more of him through you and get him to drop me a line himself. Try to find out (on the side) what Bn he came from and how long he was at the front, what part of the line he was in, etc.? He says he came from the 1ˢᵗ Bn, but he couldn't have come over with them as he made that canoe trip after I had enlisted, didn't he? The 3ʳᵈ battle of Ypres was in the beginning of June not April

I was much surprised to get a letter from Lt. Paul Garneau the other night. He is with the 22ⁿᵈ; it will be pretty hard for me to see him as when we are out of the trenches, he is in. I also heard from Cecil who is in England. It doesn't take long now before they get out, does it? Charley Garneau must still be in England. Gee, Stell, I wish you were here to play this old piano we have in the YMCA. There is somebody trying his best just at present, but oh what a racket! Wait till I get back. We will have our old time concerts every night; sing every song that was ever printed.

How is old Martha? Tell her I am still waiting for that letter of hers she promised to write.

We have better news of the Somme fighting today. Another 5 thousand prisoners. It must be terrible there. The mud must be up to their necks. Our last week in the trenches was a very good one, no rain, and nice moonlit nights. So, patrolling was easy. Today the weather is pretty cold, but so long as it is dry I don't mind. I have just had a great feed, bought steak and tomatoes and had them fried at a house with chips. Gee, some meal! So, you see the money was received o.k.

Our Colonel has left us. He has a command in England. Don't know just what it is yet. I guess we have about 3 of our original officers now and only one of those has been out all the time.

We will be out of the trenches this Christmas and in New Year's. Don't forget to send some parcels, love to everyone,

Your brother,

Leo

Lens/Arras

December 1ˢᵗ, 1916

Dear Mama:

Received your letter of the 12ᵗʰ, and Stella's of the 8ᵗʰ, the day before yesterday and you have had snow already. Rather early this year, isn't it? But I don't suppose it will last.

We are having very cold weather but it's much more dry than last year and that's a blessing.

I get The Standard quite regularly and also The Graphic. The Standard always has some very good pictures of the front, especially in November 4ᵗʰ issue they are perfect. The sugar refinery and that railway and a number of others, they would be very nice to keep. I received all your letters; also it's a good way to number them. Then you are always sure. It's too bad about Mr. LeGros. There are so many have died since I have left, but he may get over it yet.

It's just as well you gave old Boatswain away. He was no good without Ponto, and only trouble.

I am looking forward to the box you sent. I hope it comes around Christmas time, as I don't suppose I won't get any leave until after Christmas.

I am anxiously waiting for a letter in reply to mine of October 24ᵗʰ. It seems such along time to get an answer. But I suppose it will be your next letter.

Yesterday I had a pass for the day and went back to a little town, had quite a good day, all sorts to eat and some beautiful French pastry. It was a very nice little place. Reminded me of civilization again.

When is Bert going to write again? Isn't he going for a good trip in the woods this year?

*Bye-by Mama, dear. With all good wishes
for a happy Christmas, in case I haven't a chance to
write again, and with love to all,*

Your loving son,

Leo

London, England

December 20th, 1916

Dear Stella:

*I am now in London and having the time of
my life! Arrived on the night of the 15th and have till
Christmas morning. I am going out to the Hodgsons
Christmas Eve and will remain till the day after
Boxing Day.*

*Have seen Alma and we ran out to Shorncliffe
Sunday and saw Cecil. When we came home we saw
Geoffrey had just arrived on leave. I am going down
to Herbert Pimm's office in the morning and see how
things are going with him.*

*I went down to the Pay Office today to see
about my Medal but it has not been received yet. So
when it arrives I am having it sent home addressed to
Papa.*

*Have been to see 3 shows and tonight we have
tickets for Adelphi Theater this afternoon we also
went to the Grafton Galleries and saw the Canadian
pictures. If they are shown in Montreal she must run
and see them.*

*Bye bye. Love to all and hoping you all will
have a Merry Christmas.*

Lovingly,

Leo

Lens/Arras

Jan. 3rd, 1917

I got your letter written to Ale House when I arrived that evening.

Dear Mrs. Hodgson;

I am so sorry not to have written before, to thank you for all your kindness, I did enjoy my two day stay with you all so much and it was pretty hard to leave all the comforts of home for this awful life again, but never mind since I am back with the boys and settled down to work again things look much better and it's not so awful after all.

Everything has been ok I caught the train from Victoria the following morning and was delayed one day, on landing next afternoon we took the train to xxxxxx and went into the trenches the following night. We are now back in reserve again, as muddy as ever I was.

I was so pleased I brought that parcel with me, I would have starved only for that and the turkey and cake was so good.

I received your box only today, it has been a long time on the way and Jim's long letter and drawing enclosed, I also received you letter of the 27th and Mary's enclosed. I am anxiously looking forward for the calendar she has painted me.

My cold is ever so much better now I don't think dry clothes and soft beds agree with me.

With love to all and a Happy New Year,

Leo

Vimy Area

February 10th, 1917

Dear Stella:

I have not had a letter from home since my last letter to you. But it must be due to the boats. I hope all the letters don't go to the bottom. What do you people think of the USA? Are they really going to do something?

I am afraid our rest is finished and we will be going back to the line in a day or two. It will be as bad as coming back off leave again. The day before yesterday the Div held a Bn Scout contest. The 7 men of each Scout section were taken out to a certain map location and told the enemy was entrenched along a railroad track from map location such and such. A plan to such a place we had to draw a map with a report giving full information needed so that the Bn could be drawn up and make an attack at once. We are still waiting results. The first prize is 90 francs and our officer has promised 100 cigarettes each. I hope we win it.

I have been going about with Dick Luce quite a lot this last week. He has a fine job, has had two leaves since over here, and is away back from the line.

The weather is still very cold. The French people tell us they haven't had a winter like this for 20 years. But there should soon be a break now.

Yesterday I received a little parcel from Mrs. Hodgson. She has a house full of sickness, mumps and measles. She has been nursing since Christmas. I am enclosing a picture of Dick and myself. He looks terribly thin in the picture, but is nothing like that. I have a big pair of gloves on and my hands look an awful size.

I also have some Vic's Patrols to send out,
but have to put stamps on them that are hard to get.
But I will try to get them away today. I haven't any
more news today. My next letter will be from the line
again, I guess. Hoping you are all well, and that the
Hun submarines won't starve you out. They seem to
think they are going to do wonders.

With much love to all and hoping to hear from
you soon,

Leo

Vimy Area

February 17ᵗʰ, 1917

Dear Mums:

Just a line as it's already quite a few days
since my last letter. I haven't heard from home or
Canada yet. Can't make out where my mail can be
going, but everybody is the same. So, I suppose it will
all turn up some time. We are in the line again and
the weather is much warmer. We have a very com-
fortable dugout. Patrolling is a bit difficult but very
interesting.

I saw Edgar Beaupre before coming in. We
were quite near one another when I am out on rest. I
will also be able to look up some of the Gaspé boys.
Will write longer next time.

With much love,

Leo

P.S. Have just read two letters from home, Lauretta's
number 4 from January 14ᵗʰ and Marion's 15ᵗʰ
January 22ⁿᵈ. So, none have been lost. The money en-
closed was also thankfully received. Also had a letter
from Gertie of the 22ⁿᵈ.

L.

Vimy Area

Feb 18th, 1917

Did I put the wrong number on my last letter? I see you have the 402 underlined again. Surely I was not so stupid again?

  L.

Dear Mrs. Hodgson;

  The two last parcels Jan 31st & Feb 7th have been received ok the little necklaces in the first one were fine and have done very valuable work.

  We are back in the line again and have been in the trenches six days and five of those I have spent in bed in my dugout as sick as could be. I hoped at first it would develop into something but no luck I am feeling fine again today. We have a nice dugout with bunks made in it so are quite comfortable.

  I had a long letter from Gertrude who is staying with Zadie she says the children are doing very nicely and they are all well and happy.

  I haven't done anything yet about what we were speaking of when I was on leave as some were ahead of me and I was waiting till their papers were through, but, it appears they have all been held up for a few months as the Canadians are going to have their own Corps so I haven't done anything. I think I might as well wait until the next smash up and then see what luck will bring. I really believe I am too lazy to do anything.

  The weather has been much warmer and we have lost all the snow again, I suppose we will be blessed with mud now until everything dries up.

I am enclosing a little snap which is not very good, I should not have left my gloves on as my hands look the size of shovels and I haven't the "gal-blimey" hat you asked for as I lost it the first week back. No you won't have the hands of the feet either as I have cut them off. Will try and get a better one some time soon.

Tell old Jim if he isn't well when you get this letter I don't know what I will do to him when I go over again.

With much love and thanks for the parcels.

Leo.

Vimy Area

February 26ᵗʰ, 1917

Dear Lauretta:

I have received all your letters at last. Number 4, 5 and 6, yours, Marion's and Mama's, our mails are being delayed all the time now, but as long as they all get here, I suppose we must be satisfied.

I see you have been having a lot of snow. Our little bit has all disappeared again, and we are mud to our knees. I had an awful time trying to keep my boots on last night. I would hold on to the tops and pull one leg along after the other, and then they got so heavy I could hardly get along. But another month and things will be drying up.

I had a good laugh over your upset at Follys. It reminded me of the Christmas I upset Gertie and Zadie into the water. Do you remember that? And I see you have the rink going again. I am afraid though there are not many people in Gaspé to skate.

Is Jack Nist also in the Pay Office? A pretty poor crowd, eh? They might just as well remain home and let a good man come across.

I was pleased to hear Sidney Carter had the M.M. I am sure John was quite pleased. It sometimes takes a very long time for these medals to go through. I know in our Bn fellows were recommended (words censored) in April and nothing was heard again till September on our way back from (censored) and then most of them were either killed or wounded.

Olga has come home again, I see. Give her my love. She wrote to me some time ago, but I haven't had time to answer it yet.

I was very surprised to hear Mrs. Amy had died. I wrote to her on the 6th of January. I wonder if she ever got it. When you get more particulars, don't forget to let me know them.

Good bye again, and with love to all, hoping this will soon all be over, and I will be back with you all again.

Your loving brother,

Lills

Vimy Area

March 21st, 1917

Dear Mrs. Hodgson:

Thanks so much for the parcels of Feb 28th, March 7th and 14th. The latter I received last night. Your letter of the 7th I can't find anywhere and I have forgotten what you told me to call you aunt – such a memory I have.

The chap who was with me in that picture with the elephant gloves is what we call a bomb proofer, is in Corps H.Q. and never seen the trenches or been closer than ten miles I suppose, so you see is not a poor fellow at all, I suppose they suffer with their cold feet tho. When they think they might be sent up the line anyway he will never get an egg from me.

Isn't the news great both on this front and Mesopotamia? I wonder how long it will take us to drive them out of their new position? I hope not as long as the last.

I would give anything to have a talk with some of the inhabitants who were captured in Roye. Well let's hope we keep them flying till we reach Berlin. I wish the Turks were here instead of Fritz he seems to run more easily.

My cold has been quite all gone for about two days but I don't know how long it will stay away, the pine tablets are not so bad and I believe did away with the cough.

I had a long letter from home last night and the mean censor had to open it. It's the first letter I have received which has been censored and I have been swearing ever since.

With much love to Mary and Jim. Ask Jim how that 75 gun of his is shooting.

Yours,

Leo.

PART III

❦

Vimy Ridge

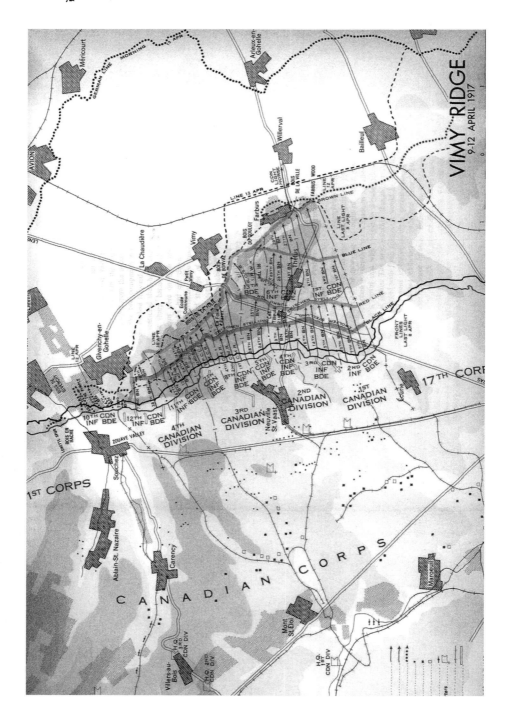

CHAPTER 9

The Battle of Vimy Ridge

The taking of Vimy Ridge by the Canadian Corps in April 1917 has taken on mythic proportions for Canadians—at least for English speaking Canadians. Moreover, the significance attached to this first major military action undertaken by Canadians alone is understood by many to be the singular moment when Canada became a nation.

The sub-surface ground under Vimy Ridge is chalk, which had for millenniums been tunneled into for various reasons. Huguenots had sheltered from religious persecution in rooms dug into the soft chalk hundreds of years earlier. When the war came both sides dug their way underground. The British dug below so they could plant huge caches of ammonal under German installations that were then exploded killing everybody above ground and leaving huge craters. Survivors of the gigantic blast scrambled to occupy the new hole in the ground. Sometimes the British won; sometimes the Germans. And sometimes both sides won—each side occupying the opposite side of the same crater.

One part of the plan for the Canadian assault on Vimy Ridge called for the construction of access tunnels from behind the Canadian lines to, and sometimes beyond into "no man's land." The tunnels enabled Canadian troops to advance in safety for as long as possible before emerging above ground to face the enemy in the open.

One tunnel, "The Grange," was more than a mile in length, 25 feet under ground, with communication rooms for headquarters staff, and thousands of troops waiting quietly underground immediately before zero hour. Local residents reported that after the war you could walk underground using ancient and modern tunnels for ten miles in that area. It is still possible to walk some of these tunnels today.

The Canadian Corps lined up from south to north in numerical order. In a four-mile front the undulations of Vimy Ridge dictated uneven sectors for each of the Divisions taking part. The First Division had a wide front for its jumping off point that narrowed as the men moved up the hill. The Second Division, on their left, had a narrow front as its jumping off point that widened as it progressed up the hill. The Third and Fourth Divisions had straight sectors but with high hills to overcome.

Exiting from the Zivy cave, the 24th Victoria Rifles were led by Leo and his fellow Scouts. They wore green armbands for identification as they escorted the second line of the Brigade into open ground to begin their advance.

Leo and the Scouts passed through the leaders at the point of the first objective. Here the leaders consolidated their positions and, as they did so, the Battalion began spreading out across the widening front. Both the right and left of the line bore off on a slant to maintain contact with the First Division on their right and the Third on their left.

Most of the Second Division's casualties occurred here—as the line expanded and met a fully aroused enemy who had yet to feel the brunt of the creeping barrage. Leo sheared off to the left just ahead of the Black Line, the 24th's first objective.

As planned, the Second Division within which the 24th Battalion Victoria Rifles was part, took each of its objectives in the time table allotted and was on the Arras railway embankment on the plain beyond the ridge when relieved six days later.

The Second Division, like the First Division had, an easier fight than the Third, who nevertheless caught-up to the overall schedule before day's end. Only the Fourth had not completed their first day's assignment, but this was achieved the following day.

The Canadian Corps' victory at Vimy surprised Allied military experts because the Canadians inflicted such a complete and utter rout of a first-class German force entrenched in the high ground since 1914. Previous attacks on Vimy Ridge by both French and British forces failed to dislodge the Germans. In contrast, the Canadian action was a tactical "tour de force" executed flawlessly by a well-trained and confident army.

Nonetheless, the taking of the Vimy Ridge did not win the war. It was planned to be no more than a supporting part of a larger strategic initiative undertaken by British forces on the River Scarpe, and General Nivelle's French plan to break out of the stalemate existing on the Western Front. The British and Canadian forces achieved their limited objectives—but the French were unable to make the hoped for breakthrough.

Because there were no plans to exploit a possible Canadian success, the Canadians were forced to halt on the far side of Vimy—even as the Germans fled across the Douai plain in front of them. But in 1918 Vimy Ridge was still in Allied hands and its commanding position was significant in the defeat of Germany's last-ditch attempt to mount an offensive campaign.

The larger strategic initiative failed. The French returned to their original line and the Germans scrambled to perfect new defensive positions. Both General Nivelle for the French, and General Falkenhausen the Commander of Germany's 6th Army, were replaced. Meanwhile, Julian Byng was promoted to General and given the command of the Third British Army. Arthur Currie was promoted to Lt. General and was given command of the Canadian Corps in Byng's place in June 1917.

The Official British History of the Vimy action places it in the context of the overall strategic plan of which it was a part. This was called The Battle of the Scarpe. In contrast, Canadian historians have devoted volumes to both The Battle of Vimy Ridge and its significance for Canada.

The official end of the Vimy action was April 14th and The Canadian Corps was relieved on the 16th. Within the context of WWI, the number of Canadian casualties at The Battle of Vimy Ridge could be considered light—yet the more than 10,000 men killed or wounded confirms that Canada's success at Vimy Ridge was not a walkover. The Victoria Rifles lost 40% of the battalion in this battle.

CHAPTER 10

Leo's Vimy

A frontline soldier during WWI had little chance of surviving un-harmed. Allied forces suffered fifty-percent casualties. These casualties came from the one-third of soldiers in harm's way at any point in time—the remaining soldiers being in reserve, at rest, or in non-combat roles. A frontline soldier rotating into the trenches, with only one leave per year for other ranks, or four per year for officers, was from a statistical point of view in a very bad way. Leo served as a frontline soldier from September 1915 to April 1917—a very long run.

On the 24th Battalion's Victoria Rifles' return in 1919 the nominal role, by my count, listed only 3 of the 42 officers and only 38 of the 1,089 "other ranks" whose names had appeared on the embarkation role. The difference was the result of transfers, reassignments, and by far the most significant—the casualty list

Col. Gunn, who had returned earlier, came up from Toronto to greet the remains of his former Command. This day there was no obstruction by boisterous and fervent bystanders as there had been when the 24th departed for England. The group of almost 900 men (many of whom who had been attached to the unit only for the trip home) had a brief official ceremony at the railway station from which the public was excluded. They marched without special notice directly to their barracks on Peel Street. The following day the 24th Battalion was disbanded. Everyone returned home.

৪০

Leo died at 2 a.m. on April 18th, 1917, aged 23, at the base hospital at Wimereux on the coast of France. He died from wounds received on the morning of April 9th during the first assault on Vimy Ridge.

Eyewitness accounts report that Leo was shot 100 yards beyond the "Black Line" where the 24th was to have stopped its initial assault.

ೲ

Leo is buried in the Wimereux Communal Cemetery in a section reserved for war dead—Plot II, Row H, Grave 10. Canadian, British and even some German soldiers are buried with him in the beautifully maintained cemetery. A few feet away from Leo's grave is the grave of Colonel John McCrae who wrote *"In Flanders Fields,"* the poem revered by Canadians as best capturing the feelings of those who fought in the Great War.

ೲ

IN FLANDERS FIELDS

IN FLANDERS FIELDS THE POPPIES BLOW
BETWEEN THE CROSSES ROW ON ROW,
THAT MARK OUR PLACE; AND IN THE SKY
THE LARKS, STILL BRAVELY SINGING, FLY
SCARCE HEARD AMID THE GUNS BELOW.

WE ARE THE DEAD. SHORT DAYS AGO
WE LIVED, FELT DAWN, SAW SUNSET GLOW,
LOVED AND WERE LOVED, AND NOW WE LIE
IN FLANDERS FIELDS.

TAKE UP OUR QUARREL WITH THE FOE:
TO YOU FROM FAILING HANDS WE THROW
THE TORCH; BE YOURS TO HOLD IT HIGH.
IF YE BREAK FAITH WITH US WHO DIE
WE SHALL NOT SLEEP, THOUGH POPPIES GROW
IN FLANDERS FIELDS.

— John McCrae

EPILOGUE

DAILY MAIL
April 25ᵗʰ, 1917

PAYS SUPREME SACRIFICE

Word was received from Ottawa last night, that Pte. Leo B. LeBoutillier, son of Mr. C. Sutton LeBoutillier of Gaspé Harbour, Quebec, who was wounded on the battlefield, died as a result of his wounds. Pte. LeBoutillier had been fighting in France for some time, and was known to be one the most courageous men on the battlefront.

ℰℴ

France
27.4.17

Mr. C. S. LeBoutillier
Gaspé

Dear Mr. LeBoutillier:

Please accept my deepest sympathy at the loss of your very gallant son. I was in England with Trench Fever when he was hit, but Mr. Bushe was with him and is going to write you and give you full particulars. I feel his loss is not only one to his Battalion and his Country but also a very real personal one. The whole time he has been in the

Battalion he has been an example of devotion to duty and gallantry. We were at the Somme fighting together and his bravery and gallantry there was simply magnificent. His "Distinguished Conduct Medal" was won three and four times over.

A few weeks ago he was recommended for a Commission. He would have made a splendid Officer—he was familiarly known as "Boots" by all his comrades and by his death the Battalion loses one of the finest men it ever had. Please express my deepest sympathy to all his family and believe me,

Your Sincerely

Lt. Colonel R.O. Alexander
Commanding 24ᵗʰ Battalion, Canadians

France
28.4.17

Dear Mr. LeBoutillier:

I have just been told that your son, Private L.B. LeBoutillier has died of wounds and I want to express my sincerest sympathy and tell you how we all feel for you in the loss of such a fine boy. Your son was wounded on the 9ᵗʰ of April during the Advance. His wounds were severe and we were afraid he would not pull through, but as he was rushed through the Dressing Station and from there to a General Hospital, we began to feel that he was winning out. I am unable to give you any particulars as to his death but I thought you would like to know that a few weeks ago I had the pleasure of signing a recommendation for his promotion to the commissioned ranks. Had the boy survived he would have got his commission. I don't know a more popular man in the Battalion than

*your son. He won his D.C.M. for conspicuous bravery
last fall. He has done most valuable work ever since
he has been in France and indeed we all shall miss
him greatly. You have the heartfelt sympathy of every
Officer and man who ever came in contact with him.*

*Very Sincerely yours,
C.F. Ritchie, Major.*

May 9ᵗʰ, 1917

Dear Zadie:

*This hasty note will bring you enclosed copy of a
letter written by the Commanding Officer of Leo's
Regiment dated the 17ᵗʰ April. It is some slight con-
solation to know his Colonel esteemed him so highly.
The copy was sent to me by the Hon. Judge Doherty to
whom the letter was addressed. With deep sympathy I
am your affectionate cousin.*

Henry J. Kavanaugh

France

17.4.17.

*The Hon. C.J. Doherty
Minister of Justice
Canada*

Dear Mr. Doherty:

*In reply to your letter regarding Pte.
LeBoutillier, he is undoubtedly an excellent soldier. I have had him in my*

*mind's eye for some time. He was with
me personally at the Somme and his
D.C.M. was magnificently won. He was
recommended for his Commission about
a month ago but I am exceedingly sorry
to say he was wounded in the groin a few
days ago. I sincerely hope he will recover
and owing to his excellent habits there is
every reason to hope for the best. If there
is anything I can do for him I shall be
delighted to and if any of his relatives
care to write to me about him.*

Yours Sincerely,

*R.O. Alexander, Lt. Col. O.C. 24th
Bn. Victoria Rifles of Canada
B.E.F. France*

May 18th, 1917

Dear Mrs. Hodgson:

*I feel that having visited you down at Westcliff last
October when on leave I am bound to write a few
lines to you concerning Leo. No doubt by this time
you have heard the sad news concerning his death.
Perhaps the details would interest his parents in
Canada if you communicate with them.*

*It seems that after leaving the jumping off
trench we had a distance of several hundred yards
to go before we stopped to consolidate which was just
beyond a main line German trench. In the heat of
excitement a good number severed off to the left and
went beyond the objective. They, of course, had to
retire for the time being until our barrage lifted and
Leo was last seen fit just a little distance in advance
of the trench that was our objective.*

Shortly afterwards he was wounded as you perhaps know, in the stomach whether by a shrapnel ball or bullet doesn't seem quite clear as the wound was a clean one and on that account hopes were entertained that if he could be got out he would stand a good chance of pulling through. His naturally strong constitution being a great asset in his favour. I can assure you everything was done to get him out as quickly as possible as he was very popular amongst the boys. But as events proved afterwards the wound proved fatal and we hear he lived only 8 days.

As was his usual temperament, when the fighting was thickest he was well to the front and I am sure, had he lived, he would have added to his reputation of being the right man for any responsible but dangerous undertaking. Perhaps you did not know, he had been offered a Commission before he went in on the 9th of April but he refused for the time being – more for appearances sake, as perhaps he thought some might possibly construe things the wrong way when a big scrap was coming off.

I was down to a town where he had a month's rest last January and the people there were very much affected when they heard he had "gone under". Without flattery or exaggeration his quick ways made him popular wherever he went amongst any people. I think I can safely say his place in the Section will be very hard to fill, even if we get the best of men.

He had two qualities combined that are very essential to carrying out the work successfully and that was character and courage. I think that you will admit they are getting rarer commodities every day. There have been a few parcels of food come lately and we have divided them up amongst the Section. I am sure that it was as he would wish.

Yours Sincerely,

–Percy D. Fuller

C. Stuart
Captain & Chaplain
24th Bn.

France May 23rd, 1917

Mr. C.S. LeBoutillier
Gaspé, P.Q.

Dear Sir.

I don't know whether anyone has already written to you about the death of your son, Pte L.B. LeBoutillier, 65553 of this Bn, but I thought I would like to add a word in any case as I had known & admired your son for over a year.

He was wounded while out on a scouting expedition in front of our lines the afternoon after we made our advance at Vimy Ridge. Apparently a German sniper caught sight of him and shot him the bullet entering his back & penetrating the abdomen. He was brought straight down to us in the dressing station and was fully conscious; all he seemed to worry about was that he was giving us some trouble. We hoped against hope that he would recover, bracing ourselves with the thought a bullet makes a clean wound and it was a sad blow to us all to hear that he had succumbed to his injuries on April 18th at no.14 General Hospital.

As to his qualities as a soldier, his actions speak for themselves. There was no more popular or more merited reward than his D.C.M for his splendid work at the Somme. He was always found in dangerous places, going about his work with the utmost coolness, an example of bravery that every one saw and recognized.

When he was brought in wounded, I held him up while the Doctor dressed his wounds, & after we had put him down on the stretcher again, I turned around to the four scouts who had carried him down

*and found them all practically in tears. They all had
the same lament. "If only it could have been someone
else not Boots" He was the idol of the boys in his section, and it wasn't altogether his bravery that won
their hearts. He was such a thorough gentleman.
Always cheerful always ready to do anything & a
clean honourable boy at all times.*

*I remember censoring a letter he wrote to the
brother of a boy who had been killed beside him at
the Somme and thinking then what a splendid letter
it was feeling sympathy & affection for the chap who
had gone.*

*And that is what I want you to understand
about your son. We are absolute feeling sympathy in
your loss, out of affection for him.*

*No one cannot but feel that he was ready to go.
His whole life was one of service whether it was for
his country or his God. And as Christ received him
into Paradise I feel so more that he returned him with
the words " well done thou good and faithful servant"
enter thou into the joy of the Lord. For that is just
what he had rendered "good and faithful service"*

*I trust all is family will know what universal
esteem & affection we all had for him, and that the
thought of his noble example will be a solace to you
in your sorrow. Meanwhile may God and his Blessed
Mother, who knows what it was to lose her Son on the
Cross comfort you.*

*His personal effects will be sent to you through
the official channels which are however exceedingly
slow. Also if you desire any information regarding
his death or where he is buried I should advise you
to write to the R.C. Chaplain no.14 General Hospital
B.E.F France.*

With my deepest sympathy believe me.

Faithfully yours,

*C. Stuart
Captain and Chaplain 24th Can. Bn. BEF*

જી

"Was the WWI worth the sacrifice," is a question asked in many accounts of this war. The last line of Pierre Berton's "Vimy" answers in a simple "no."

But this is entirely too simple an answer. Leo's letters demonstrate that, insofar as the individual is concerned, the question is irrelevant. A sacrifice for the individual is the price paid for membership in the society of his choice.

Leo had no doubt that his life in Gaspé was of great value to him. Leo writes home often and always from the focus of the home front, almost never involving his correspondents in the horrors he was experiencing. Leo maintains the reality of life at home while living an unreal existence in France.

Leo recognized where he was and what part he was expected to play, even though his "expectations" at sign-up and the "facts" as he found them on the battlefield were at such great variance. He does not blame others for his situation and accepts responsibility for his own decisions—even when the results for him are terrible. Leo used his intelligence to survive in one of human history's worst killing zones and in this he was for many months highly successful. When his options ran out Leo simply did his duty.

APPENDIX A

CANADIAN INFANTRY
DISTINGUISHED CONDUCT MEDAL
No. 65553 PRIVATE, L. B. LeBOUTILLIER

FOR CONSPICUOUS GALLANTRY IN ACTION

HE CARRIED OUT A RECONNAISSANCE UNDER VERY HEAVY FIRE, OBTAINING MOST VALUABLE INFORMATION. LATER HE RESCUED A WOUNDED MAN, AND CARRIED OUT SEVERAL MORE DARING RECONNAISSANCES, ALSO CARRYING BOMBS AND AMMUNITION TO THE FRONT LINE. HE DISPLAYED GREAT COURAGE AND DETERMINATION THROUGHOUT.

LONDON GAZETTE No, 29824
NOVEMBER 14TH, 1916

౭ఎ

The Distinguished Conduct Medal was awarded for acts of gallantry to "other ranks" and was first awarded in 1854 during the Crimean War. The D.C.M. was regarded as second only to the Victoria Cross. During the early years of the First World War there were so many circumstances where the originally conceived D.C.M. would be warranted, it was decided to create the Military Medal (M.M) in the spring of 1916, to be awarded for "gallantry." The D.C.M. would thenceforth only be awarded for "exceptional gallantry." Leo's D.C.M. was awarded in November 1916 placing him in a small group recognized for exceptional gallantry. During the First World War, 600,000 Canadians served, and 1,947 were awarded the D.C.M.

APPENDIX B

LEO'S OVERSEAS LOCATIONS DURING SERVICE WITH THE 24TH VICTORIA RIFLES

1. Arrival in England, Southampton, May 20th, 1915

2. Sandling Camp

3. Shorncliffe, RAMC Hospital, May 30th to July 5th

4. Sandling Camp, July 6th to September 15th

5. Arrival in France, Boulogne, September 16th, 1915

6. St. Omer, September 17th

7. Bailleul, September 21st

8. Locre, Kemmel Front, September 23rd, 1915 to April 2nd, 1916

9. Ypres Sector (St Eloi Craters), April 16th to May 30th, 1916

10. Zillebeke, May 28-30th to August 24th

11. The Somme, August 24th to October 3rd, 1916, marching through:
    a. Steervoode, August 26th
    b. Noorpeene, August 27th
    c. Eperlecques, August 28th
    d. Arques, September 4th
    e. Conteville, September 5th
    f. Coulonvillers, September 5th
    g. Halloy Les Pernois, September 6th
    h. La Vicogne, September 7th
    i. Herissart, September 8th
    j. Arriving at Courcelette, September 9th to October 3rd 1916

12. October 4th to October 14th, marching through:
   a. Bertaucourt
   b. Hem
   c. Bonnieres
   d. Houvin
   e. Ostervilles
   f. Maisnil Les Ruitz
   g. Arriving at Bully Grenay, Oct 15th
      to January 16th, 1917

13. Bruay, January 17th to March 11th, 1917

14. Vimy, March 23rd, 1917 to April 9th, 1917

15. Dressing and casualty clearing station,
   April 9th to April 16th, 1917

16. Wimereux Field Hospital April 16th to April 18th, 1917

APPENDIX C

An article written by Leo describing a moose hunt published in
ROD AND GUN MAGAZINE
1910

A Hunt in Gaspé
by L.B.L.B.

On the first of September, nineteen hundred and ten, we were ready to leave on our first hunting trip. We were a party of four and all anxious to get into the woods and see what real sport was like.

Five o'clock in the morning all were up and waiting for the guide and driver. At six thirty we were off, four of us ahead with a horse and carriage, while behind were the guide and driver with the heavy truck horse conveying the provisions.

The first part of the road followed the Gaspé Bay to its head, a distance of about seven miles. Then we switched to another road that turned toward the West and followed the York River for thirty miles.

We followed this road until we came to Fourth Lake crossing. Here we stopped and got out the necessaries for our first meal, which consisted of tea and canned goods.

After dinner we forded the river and walked for three miles to Fourth Lake. Three of us went ahead, one with .44 and the other two with a .22 each hoping to get a shot at partridge. Our luck however was poor and we were nearly eaten alive by the flies.

Finally we reached the lake. We had now ceased to talk above a whisper, for fear we should disturb any moose that might be lying around. Noiselessly we crept to the water's edge.

It is a beautiful lake, a mile long and three quarters of a mile wide. Here and there we could see wild ducks, geese and other wild fowl. We resisted the temptation to fire as a shot among the lakes in this district with steep mountains surrounding them would have echoed and re echoed for miles around. Walking quietly back to the cabin we got supper ready, cut green boughs and got everything in order for the night.

Just about sunset we took the punt and poled slowly along the lakeshore heading for a green patch on the other side. With the field glasses we were soon able to distinguish a fine buck moose eating the leaves of an alder tree. Before long he walked slowly back into the woods. On reaching the other side we sat quietly, listening for about twenty minutes during which time nothing occurred to break the stillness. Then a crackling of dry leaves was heard not far away.

"There they come," whispered the guide as the sound grew nearer. Now there plunged splashing into the waters of the creek two large moose and a younger one. Quietly they stood and the guide whispered, "Shoot!" I was to have first chance, so taking aim at the one with the biggest head I quickly fired two shots. The big animal turned then stumbled and fell.

In the meantime another one of our party had knocked over the other large moose.

The smallest one was still on his feet but no one wanted to take a shot at him; he was too small and not worthwhile taking out. At the same time he was not too small to give us considerable trouble. I tried to get out of the punt to finish up my old buck who was still kicking but the younger one kept dangerously near me and ready to charge. It was not safe to land and at last we decided to have one keep him covered while the other got closer and finished up the two moose.

As I was coming back and only a few yards from the punt, the young moose charged. He pretty nearly knocked me over but I was able to get into the punt safely while the guide held him off with the paddle. He seemed determined we should not get on shore again and followed us around the lake trotting along in the water. At last we dodged him and got on the other side of the lake first where we succeeded in getting a lot of stones. With these we were able to beat him off whenever he came near and at last he gave up the fight while we skinned the moose and cut them up in quarters.

No sooner was everything ready to put into the punt and return to camp than our troubles began afresh. The young moose reappeared and was in a combative humor. However, we managed to keep him off until the meat, skins and heads were loaded.

We then paddled pack to camp and before we had everything straightened up for the night it was past twelve o'clock.

The following morning after breakfast we started across the lake again so see if our friend of the night before had left.

We found him still in possession and as plucky as ever. No one bothered him this time and we all succeeded in getting some good pictures.

After dinner we separated, going in different directions in search of partridge. We got an average of ten each and that night dined royally on moose steak and partridge. Hunting stories around a cheery campfire followed and we rolled into our bunks.

The morning of the third day we packed up and started for North West Lake that is at the head of the Dartmouth River. The truck was sent back with the meat and the carriage continued on with us to "Twenty-eight Camp".

Here we spent the night in our tent as there was no log cabin. All went to bed early as we had a long rough trail to follow the next day.

In the morning we awoke to find it was pouring rain. This decided us to remain over another day as our things would have been in an awful state had we carried our packs through the woods in a rainstorm. We slept the greater part of the day, going for a walk in the woods in the afternoon to help pass the time.

All was ready next morning and we were off at seven thirty, each carrying a pack of sixty pounds weight. The first part of the trail was up steep mountain road about a mile and half long. We were all feeling shaky when we reached the top and stopped to rest ten minutes. My carrying strap, which was across my chest had been causing a sharp pain that caught me at every breath and I was forced to change it to the back of my neck and under my arms.

We resumed the trail which was hard to follow as it is very seldom traveled in early Fall, and in consequence was not very well blazed. By twelve o'clock all were laboring under the packs and were very tired. Soon after however we reached our destination and had a bite to eat.

Then having pitched our camp we started again towards the lake. As we were now on the flat lands where moose and caribou feed we were on the alert.

We did not see the lake until we had reached it then it burst suddenly upon us in the bushes. We walked out onto a little peninsula but saw nothing and as we did not intend calling until the last day, we returned to camp and had dinner and a little rest.

About three thirty we again betook ourselves to the lake. We waited a long time in silence. Then we heard something slowly walking along. Two minutes passed. Then a beautiful cow moose and calf came into view.

We did not trouble her but lying low amongst the small trees watched her paddle about and feed among the lilies for about an hour or so. She was a beauty and the guide said she was the best he had ever seen. She finally scented us, and looking up quickly, gazed around and then turning, made towards the woods.

As it was then sunset we returned to camp.

The morning of the fourth found us at the lake just as the sun was rising. It was not long before we heard a splash and looking up quickly saw a caribou standing in water to his knees.

This was Albert's shot and taking good aim he brought down the caribou with a bullet to the shoulder and we then ran quickly round the lake to the place where he was lying. He was still alive but a .22 bullet that I put through his forehead finished him and he dropped like a stone.

We had got a rare head this time. The skin of the caribou was unusually dark and its horns were still covered with a short or skin and fur that gave them a beautiful appearance. We all helped the guide to skin him and then carried everything to camp.

An early dinner followed and we started with our load over the trail, the guide carrying the head and skin and each of us a quarter. We aimed to take it out to the top of the mountain a distance of five miles and return this afternoon.

Carrying the packs along at a good pace as we were all getting used to the work, we did not mind the loads so made good time and beat our trip in by an hour.

Coming back it poured with rain and we arrived at the camp at half past six drenched to the skin.

We were to leave the next morning. Returning to the lake the guide put the birch horn that he had brought with him to his mouth and after giving a long bawl listened.

Again he tried and in ten seconds we heard a sort of grunt that was followed by the crackling sound made by limbs when a big animal is taking a little run. Then this stopped and we heard another grunt. All were in great excitement but not till half an hour had passed were we able to discern a large bull at a distance of about fifty yards.

This fellow had a spread of nearly fifty-eight inches, one of the best heads any of us had ever seen.

Ten minutes passed before George got a chance to shoot. Then when he was ready the bull made a quick start and trotted along the shore. George fired and missed, then fired twice. The bull fell but was on his feet again in a second and with a leap plunged into the bushes.

By this time George, who was a poor shot, and who had a bad attack of buck fever, fired quickly, aiming at the place where the moose had disappeared. We thought the big chap must be lying around somewhere and hoped he might be dead.

We had a long way to go round the lake before we got to the place where he had disappeared and to our amazement the bull was not to be seen. After hunting for ten minutes or more we got on his track and traced him for half a mile. By the stride we could see that he was traveling at great speed and the guide said that there were no signs of being fatally wounded. This determined us to give him up, though not without great disappointment.

Returning to the camp we got everything packed up and were almost glad not to have the weight of the big bull added to our load.

The trail back was slippery and the walking heavy as a result of the previous day's rain.

We made good time notwithstanding and reached "Twenty-eight Camp" about the dinner hour. After a rest of an hour and a half we set out again to the top of the mountain for the caribou meat we had carried out the day before.

On returning we found the truck had come up for us and the story of our luck was told while the two men pitched camp for our last night in the woods.

After supper large logs were cut for a fire and we were all asleep in a minute, being fatigued after a hard day's work.

Next morning broke fine and clear for the homeward journey. Two of us walked in front and brought down fifteen partridges that we encountered in different places.

We returned to town at five o'clock in the evening all in fine spirits and greatly improved after our few days' sport in the woods.

GLOSSARY

Army: Two or more Corps (General).

B of T: The Bank of Toronto. The Gaspé Harbour branch of this Bank employed Leo prior to his enlistment.

Battalion: Three to five Companies (Lieutenant Colonel).

Blighty: England. Also, used to describe a wound severe enough to get you returned to England.

Bn: Battalion (Approximately 900 men. At the assault on Vimy Ridge, the 24th Victoria Rifles moved off numbering 784 men).

Bomb Proof: Name given to those who had jobs well back from the Front and were therefore not in danger. Frontline troops resented the "bomb proofers."

Brigade: Three to five Regiments (Brigadier General).

Company: Three to five Platoons (Captain/Major).

Corps: Two or more Divisions (Lieutenant General).

Cpl: Corporal.

Div: Abbreviation for Division. As the war progressed both sides accepted fewer and fewer men as comprising a division. By lowering the number of men comprising a division you avoided having to downgrade that unit. This meant that senior officers would not need to revert to lower rank more appropriate to the numbers of men under their command. (Canadian divisions numbered 20/22,000 men and were at or near full strength most of the time making them among the most powerful units in the Allied armies).

Division: Three to five Brigades (Major General).

Housewife: Sewing repair kit.

Hun/Fritz: The name given Germans. Newspapers were more likely to refer to Germans as Boche or Hun. The front line Canadian soldier was more likely to use Fritz a less offensive description evoking a more collegial attitude to men in a similar situation to their own.

Imperial: A member of the British Army. Most English speaking Canadians assumed they were British but chose to think of themselves as belonging to a Canadian Army rather than to the Imperial Army.

L/Cpl: Section leader.

N.C.O.: Non commissioned officer. All officers not holding the King's commission (Warrant Officer and below).

Nedra: The Leboutillier family motorboat.

Platoon: 30/60 men (Sergeant/2nd Lieutenant).

Ponto: The Leboutillier family dog, a particular friend of Leo's.

Postal: The pre-printed post card that was a short cut way to let your correspondent know how you were.

Pte: Private.

R.A.M.C.: Royal Army Medical Corps Where Leo was hospitalized on arrival in England for suspected spinal meningitis.

R.E.: The Royal Engineers were a military unit who built bridges, train tracks and designed and built defensive works.

R.S.M. -Regimental Sergeant Major.

Regiment: Two to five Battalions (Colonel).

Regt.: Abbreviation for Regiment. A Regiment was made up of two or more Battalions, consequently varied greatly in numbers.

Sometimes used interchangeably with Battalion.

Sandling: Canadian Army camp, where the Second Division trained in England prior to going to France.

Section: 10/15 men (Lance/corporal / Corporal).

Sgt.: Sergeant.

S. M.: Sergeant Major.

Trixie: The Leboutillier family carriage horse, Its partner was Maude.

W.O.: Warrant Officer, most senior non commissioned rank.

Whiz Bang: German high velocity shell (so called because of the noise it made prior to arrival and the explosion immediately following it's arrival).

RESOURCES

Aitken, Max Sir M.P. *Canada in Flanders,* Hodder & Stoughton London, 1916. Max Aitkin, later Lord Beaverbrook, was a personal friend and supporter of Sam Hughes. Given access to the front by Hughes; Aitken's 1916 account of Canada's war experience was totally candid, accurately recording failures as well as successes. Newspaper reports of the time were totally biased, reporting everything including dismal failures as great victories.

Berton, Pierre, *Vimy,* McClellan and Stewart, 1986. Berton's account of the Vimy campaign supports and reinforces the proposition that this was a defining moment for Canada in its pursuit of nationhood.

Boyden, Joseph, *Three Day Road,* Viking Canada, 2005. A psychological novel based on accurate information relative to Canadian Native Peoples participation in front line sniper activity.

Brown, Angus & Gimblett, Richard, *In The Footsteps of the Canadian Corps,* Majic Light Publishing, 2006. Featuring the Canadian War Museum collection. The Canadian contribution to military operations in France from start to finish; amply illustrated, Maps.

Christie, Norm, *For King & Empire:* Volume 2, The Canadians on the Somme, Bunker to Bunker Books, Winnipeg, 1996 . A history of The Battle of the Somme and a resource for a self guided tour of the battleground.

Drolet, Gil, *Loyola the Wars,* Wilfred Laurier University Press, 1996. Biographies of Loyola College alumni who died in Canada's wars.

Fetherstonhaugh, R.C., *The 24th Battalion,* C.E.F., Victoria Rifles of Canada 1914-1919, The Gazette Printing Company, 1930. The regimental history of the 24th Battalion. Includes details of the unit's movements, actions, statistics and personnel records. Includes maps of the unit's movements during W.W.I.

Gilbert, Martin, *The Battle of the Somme*, McClelland & Stewart, 2006. A book describing a battle which has as its most significant measurement the largest number of casualties in 138 days ever recorded in any war is not a funny book. It is however a wonderfully researched report on people and events of this incredible battle written by the celebrated official biographer of Winston Churchill.

Granatstein, J.L, *Canada's Army,* University of Toronto Press, 2002. Three hundred years of Canadian military history, nevertheless deals in great detail with the First World War. The book is especially informative in describing the 1916 actions where Leo earned his medal and lost his friends.

Gray, Charlotte, *Canada a Portrait in Letters 1800-2000,* Doubleday Canada, 2003. Contains numerous letters from the Great War period everything from letters written by Sir Robert Borden on the Canadian Governments interaction with the British conduct of the war to a letter written by Stuart Tomkins describing how a bear named Winnie from Jackknife joined the 89th Alberta Overseas Battalion as mascot and ended in a London Zoo, where A.A. Milne made him into Winnie the Pooh.

Greenhous, Brereton & Harris, Stephen J. *Canada and the Battle of Vimy Ridge,* Queens Printer, 2004. Analysis of the Vimy assault. The preparation, the operation and its aftermath.

Grescoe , Audrey and Paul, *The Book of War Letters,* McClelland & Stewart Ltd., 2003. A compilation of a hundred years of Canadian soldiers war letters, from the Boer War to Afghanistan. Much of the content is reminiscent of Leo's letters.

Hedges, Chris, *War Is a Force That Gives Us Meaning,* Anchor Books, 2003. Descriptions of the psychological challenges facing soldiers who aspire to competence in real combat.

MacDonald Cooper, Lois, *Wartime Letters Home,* Borealis Press, 2005. Second World War letters from a member of the Canadian Red Cross produced as part of a 60th anniversary of VE Day commemoration project. Letters and personal comment on the war and its conduct.

McKeane, G.B. V.C, *Scouting Thrills,* C.E.F. Books, 2003. Originally published in 1919 describes individual scouting activities in "No Man's Land."

Nicholson, G.W. Col., *Official History of the Canadian Army in the First World War: Canadian Expeditionary Force 1914-1919.* Queens Printer and Controller of Stationary, Ottawa, Canada,1962.

O'Shea, Stephen, *Back to the Front,* Walker & Company, 1996. Eighty years after W.W.I, the author traces the entire 400 miles of battlefield trenches.

Pariseau, Jean and Bernier, Serge, *French Canadians and Bilingualism in the Canadian Armed Forces, Volume 1 1763-1969 The Fear of a Parallel Army*, Directorate of History Department of National Defense, 1986. A detailed account of the struggles of the Canadian military establishment in the post WW2, implementation of the principle of "institutional bilingualism" that became Canadian Government policy.

Turner, Alexander, *Vimy Ridge 1917 Byng's Canadians Triumph at Arras*, Osprey, 2005. Written by a currently serving Officer in the British Army, this is a technically accurate and fair report. This book along with Berton's Vimy and Granatsteins Canada' Army will meet the need of the casual reader to be informed on the significance to Canada of Vimy as a military "tour de force."

PHOTO CREDITS

Schooner at the LeBoutillier Wharf, Gaspé Harbour
Courtesy Fabien Sinnett, Gaspé, Quebec

Mobilization Parade in Montreal
D.N.D. PA 004918
© Library and Archives Canada

Little Mascot Dog, "Squidge"
D.N.D. PA 030204
© Library and Archives Canada

In the Trenches
AN 19920044-242
George Metcalf Archival Collection
© Canadian War Museum

Communications Trench
AN 19920044-247
George Metcalf Archival Collection
© Canadian War Museum

Pigeon Service, The Bird Leaving the Trench
AN 19920085-303
George Metcalf Archival Collection
© Canadian War Museum

A Hair Cut
AN 19920044-061
George Metcalf Archival Collection
© Canadian War Museum

No Man's Land, based on photo by Capt. H.E. Knobel
D.N.D PA 001020
© Library and Archives Canada

All Photos of Leo Leboutillier and Family
Courtesy the Leboutillier and Pimm families

MAP CREDITS

Western Front Map and *Vimy Ridge Map*
Courtesy Nicholson, G. W. L. 1962. *Official History of the Canadian Army in the First World War: Canadian Expeditionary Force 1914-1919.* Queens Printer and Controller of Stationary, Ottawa, Canada.

ABOUT THE AUTHOR

GORDON PIMM served during World War II as a Signalman in the Royal Canadian Navy, primarily on Corvettes in the North Atlantic Convoys. Following wartime service, he earned his B.Comm. from McGill University in Montreal, Quebec. He earned his M.A. from the University of Miami, Florida. He lives in Ottawa with his wife June and his trusty West Highland White Terrier, Duncan. This is his first book.

For additional information about this book
visit the *Leo's War* website

http://www.leoswar.com

℘